THE TOWER OF DEATH

Borgo Press Books by ALEXANDRE DUMAS

Anthony
The Barricade at Clichy; or, The Fall of Napoleon
Bathilda
Caligula
The Corsican Brothers (with Eugène Grangé & Xavier de Montépin)
The Count of Monte Cristo, Part One: The Betrayal of Edmond Dantès
The Count of Monte Cristo, Part Two: The Resurrection of Edmond Dantès
The Count of Monte Cristo, Part Three: The Rise of Monte Cristo
The Count of Monte Cristo, Part Four: The Revenge of Monte Cristo
A Fairy Tale (with Adolphe de Leuven and Léon Lhérie)
The Gold Thieves (with Countess Céleste de Chabrillan)
Kean
The Last of the Three Musketeers; or, The Prisoner of the Bastille (Musketeers #3)
Lorenzino
The Mohicans of Paris
Napoléon Bonaparte
Queen Margot
Richard Darlington (with Prosper Dinaux)
Sylvandire
The Three Musketeers (Musketeers #1)
The Three Musketeers—Twenty Years Later (Musketeers #2)
The Tower of Death (with Frédéric Gaillardet)
The Two Dianas (with Paul Meurice)
Urbain Grandier and the Devils of Loudon
The Venetian
The Whites and the Blues
The Widow's Husband; and, Porthos in Search of an Outfit
Young Louix XIV

RELATED DRAMAS:

The Queen's Necklace, by Pierre Decourcelle
The Seed of the Musketeers, by Paul de Kock & Guénée (Musketeers #5)
The San Felice, by Maurice Drack
The Son of Porthos the Musketeer, by Émile Blavet (Musketeers #4)
A Summer Night's Dream, Adolphe de Leuven & Joseph-Bernard Rosier
The Widow's Husband; and, Porthos in Search of an Outfit: Two Dumasian Comedies, edited by Frank J. Morlock

THE TOWER OF DEATH

A PLAY IN FIVE ACTS

ALEXANDRE

DUMAS & FRÉDÉRIC

GAILLARDET

Translated and Adapted by Frank J. Morlock

THE BORGO PRESS
MMXIII

THE TOWER OF DEATH

Copyright © 2001, 2013 by Frank J. Morlock

FIRST BORGO PRESS EDITION

Published by Wildside Press LLC

www.wildsidebooks.com

DEDICATION

For my good friend—Rick Roberts

CONTENTS

CAST OF CHARACTERS. 9
ACT I: PHILIPPE D'AULNAY, Scene 1 11
ACT I, Scene 2 36
ACT II: MARGUERITE DE BOURGOGNE, Scene 3 . . . 54
ACT II, Scene 4. 76
ACT III: ENGUERRAND DE MARIGNY, Scene 5 95
ACT III, Scene 6 109
ACT IV: BURIDAN, Scene 7 130
ACT V: GAULTIER D'AULNAY, Scene 8. 160
ACT V, Scene 9. 175
ABOUT THE AUTHOR 189

CAST OF CHARACTERS

Buridan

Gaultier D'Aulnay

Philippe D'Aulnay

Orsini

Savoisy

King Louis X of France

De Pierrefonds

Enguerrand de Marigny

Landry

Simon

Sire Raoul

Jehan

A Guard

A Page

Marguerite de Bourgogne

Charlotte

A Veiled Woman

Pages, Guards, Servants

ACT I:
PHILIPPE D'AULNAY
SCENE 1

Orsini's tavern at the Gate of Saint Honoré seen from the interior. A dozen servants and workers at some tables to the right of the spectator; a table apart Philippe D'Aulnay writing on a parchment. He has a wine pot and goblet near him.

RICHARD

(rising)

Okay! Master Orsini, our host, Devil's Innkeeper, Poisoner! It seems we must give you all your titles before you respond.

ORSINI

What do you want? Some wine?

SIMON

(rising)

Thanks, we have enough still. It's just that Richard wants to know how your patrol, Satan, received souls this morning.

RICHARD

Or, to speak more like a Christian, how many bodies were fished from the Seine between the Tower of Nesle and Bon Hommes.

ORSINI

Three.

RICHARD

That's the count! And all three without doubt, young, noble, and handsome?

ORSINI

All three nobles—young and handsome.

RICHARD

That's the custom—all three strangers to the good city of Paris?

ORSINI

All three arrived after the eighteenth.

RICHARD

That's the rule. At least, this calamity has some good in it—since it is contrary to the plague and the monastery—it spares the peasants and falls on the gentry. It makes up for the tax and the cover. Thanks, innkeeper—that's all we wanted from you—unless in your capacity as Italian and sorcerer you intend to tell us that it is a vampire who needs such young and hot blood to prevent his own from aging and coagulating.

ORSINI

I know nothing about it.

SIMON

And why is it always below the Tower and not upstream of it, that one finds the drowned?

ORSINI

I know nothing of it.

PHILIPPE

(calling Orsini)

Master!

SIMON

You know nothing about it? Well, leave us in peace and answer the young lord who is doing you the honor of calling you.

PHILIPPE

Master!

ORSINI

Sir?

PHILIPPE

Will one of your tavern boys deliver this letter?

ORSINI

Landry! Landry!

(Landry comes forward.)

LANDRY

Here.

(He stands before Philippe while the latter seals and addresses his letter.)

ORSINI

Do what this young lord tells you.

(Orsini walks off.)

RICHARD

(grabbing Orsini by the arm)

It's all the same, master, if I were called Orsini—may God forbid—if I were Master of this Tavern—let God make it so—and if my windows opened like yours on this old Tower—may God destroy it!—I would spend one of my nights alone to listen and watch, and I guarantee that I would reply the next day to those who asked me news.

ORSINI

It is not my business. Want some wine? I am an innkeeper, not a night watchman.

RICHARD

Go to the devil!

ORSINI

Release me then.

RICHARD

Yes—that's right.

(Orsini disappears.)

PHILIPPE

(to Landry)

Listen, boy—take this money and go to the Louvre. You will ask for Captain Gaultier D'Aulnay and you will give him this letter.

LANDRY

It will be done, Milord.

(Landry leaves.)

RICHARD

Say, Jehan de Moutheny, have you seen the procession of Queen Marguerite and her two sisters—the princesses Blanche and Jeanne?

JEHAN

I believe so.

RICHARD

One doesn't have to ask where the tax went that Philip the Fair of glorious memory lived on, on the day his eldest son was made knight—Louis le Huten. I can see my thirty sous on the back of the Queen's favorite—only the billions became gold cloth, laced and decorated. Have you seen Gaultier D'Aulnay, Simon?

(Philippe raises his head and listens.)

SIMON

Holy Virgin, have I seen him—his devilish horse prances so beautifully that he put one of his hoofs on mine with as much aplomb as if he were playing with the foot of a cow and as I cried in misery, his master to quiet me gave me—

JEHAN

A gold coin.

SIMON

Yes—a blow on the head with the pommel of his sword while calling me a thief.

JEHAN

You did nothing to the horse and said nothing to the master?

SIMON

To the horse, I virtuously embedded three cuts of a knife in the rump, and he went off bleeding; as for the master, I called him a bastard and he went off swearing.

PHILIPPE

(from his seat)

Who says Gaultier D'Aulnay is a bastard?

SIMON

Me!

PHILIPPE

(throwing his goblet at Simon's head)

You lie in your throat! Tramp!

SIMON

Help me, boys.

WORKERS

(pulling their knives)

Death to the pretty boy—to the gentleman, the silk stocking.

PHILIPPE

(drawing his sword)

Now, my master, notice my sword is much longer and sharper than your knives.

SIMON

Yes, but we have ten knives against your sword.

PHILIPPE

Get back!

ALL

Kill—kill.

(They form a circle around Philippe, who parries with his sword.)

(Buridan enters, takes off his cape tranquilly, then noticing that a gentleman is defending himself against the common people he draws his sword.)

BURIDAN

Ten against one! Ten workers against a gentleman—that's five too many.

(Buridan attacks them from behind.)

ARTISANS

Murder. Help. The Police!

(They try to escape. Orsini appears.)

BURIDAN

Innkeeper to the Devil, close your doors—so that not one of these miscreants can leave to give the alarm. They were wrong.

(to the artisans)

You were wrong.

ARTISANS

Yes, Monsignor, yes.

BURIDAN

You see, we pardon them. Remain at your tables. Here is ours. Have my friend Landry bring wine.

ORSINI

He is running an errand for this young lord; I shall have the honor of serving you myself.

BURIDAN

As you wish—but hurry—

(to the Artisans)

Anyone talking over there?

ARTISANS

No, Monsignor.

PHILIPPE

By my saint, sir, you have just gotten me out of a bad scrape and I will remember it if the like occasion should befall you.

BURIDAN

Your hand?

PHILIPPE

With all my heart.

BURIDAN

Everything is said.

(Orsini brings in wine in pots.)

BURIDAN

To your health! Take two pots to these comedians so long as they drink to our health.

(to Philippe)

This the first time, my young soldier, that I have seen you in the venerable tavern of Master Orsini; are you newly arrived in the good city of Paris?

PHILIPPE

I arrived two hours ago, just in time to see the procession of Queen Marguerite.

BURIDAN

Queen? Not yet.

PHILIPPE

Queen after tomorrow—for it's the day after tomorrow that Philip the Fair arrives from Navarre to succeed his father, the King Louis X, and I have profited from his elevation to the throne to return from Flanders where I was at war!

BURIDAN

And I from Italy where I too was fighting. It appears the same cause brings us, my dear sir?

PHILIPPE

I seek my fortune.

BURIDAN

As do I. And your ways of succeeding?

PHILIPPE

For the last six months, my brother has been Captain of Queen Marguerite's guards.

BURIDAN

His name?

PHILIPPE

Gaultier D'Aulnay.

BURIDAN

Knight, you will succeed—for the Queen can refuse nothing to your brother.

PHILIPPE

So they say; and I have just written to announce my arrival and to tell him to join me here.

BURIDAN

Here in the midst of this crowd?

PHILIPPE

Look.

BURIDAN

Ah! All our gallants have disappeared. Let us continue since they leave us free.

PHILIPPE

And may I ask you your name?

BURIDAN

My name? Say rather my names. I have two of them. One from birth which is mine and which I don't bear and one of war which isn't mine but which I bear.

PHILIPPE

And which will you tell me?

BURIDAN

My war name—Buridan.

PHILIPPE

Buridan—do you know someone at court?

BURIDAN

No one.

PHILIPPE

Your resources?

BURIDAN

(striking his face then his breast)

They are here—and here—in the head and the heart.

PHILIPPE

You are counting on your good looks and love—you are right, my Knight.

BURIDAN

I count on one more thing; I am the same age and from the same country as the Queen—I was page to Duke Robert II, her father, who died assassinated. At that time the Queen and I between us didn't have the age we both have known.

PHILIPPE

What is your age?

BURIDAN

Thirty-five years.

PHILIPPE

Well?

BURIDAN

Well, since that time, there's been a secret between Marguerite de Bourgogne and myself—a secret which will either kill me or make my fortune.

PHILIPPE

(presenting his goblet to drink)

Good luck!

BURIDAN

God give it to you, my soldier.

PHILIPPE

This isn't starting badly.

BURIDAN

Ah!

PHILIPPE

Yes; today as I returned after passing the Queen's procession, I realized I was being followed by a woman. I quickened my step and she doubled hers. In a flash, she caught up with me and said, "My young lord, a woman who loves the sword finds you handsome; are you as brave as handsome; are you as confident as brave?" I replied, "I am her man so long as she's young and pretty; if not, she can go to a nunnery." The girl said, "She is young and pretty—she will wait for you this evening at sunset at the Rue Froid-Mantel. A man will approach you and say, 'Your hand?' You will show him this purse and follow him." Then she put this ring on my finger and went away. Disappeared.

BURIDAN

You are going to this rendezvous?

PHILIPPE

By my patron saint, I won't miss it.

BURIDAN

My dear friend, I congratulate you. I've been in Paris only four days more than you and except for Landry, who is an old acquaintance, I haven't met a face to which I could put a name. God's blood! I am not yet past the age or looks to have no more adventures.

(A veiled woman comes in and touches Buridan's shoulder.)

VEILED WOMAN

Lord Captain.

(Turning without tension.)

BURIDAN

What is it, gracious lady?

VEILED WOMAN

Two words—but low.

BURIDAN

Why not out loud?

VEILED WOMAN

Because there are two words to say and four ears to hear.

BURIDAN

(rising)

Well good! Take my arm, my unknown lady, and tell me these two words.

(to Philippe)

You'll allow me.

PHILIPPE

Do it.

VEILED WOMAN

A woman who loves the sword finds you handsome; are you as

brave as you are handsome; are you as bold as you are brave?

BURIDAN

I've spent twenty years at war with the Italians, the rogues I know of, I've made love for twenty years to Italian women, the trickiest sluts I know—and I've never refused either combat or a rendezvous—provided the woman is handsome.

VEILED WOMAN

She is young, she is pretty.

BURIDAN

Fine.

VEILED WOMAN

And she will await you tonight.

BURIDAN

Where, at what time?

VEILED WOMAN

At sunset—before the second tower of the Louvre.

BURIDAN

I will be there.

VEILED WOMAN

A man will approach you and say, 'Your hand'—you will show

him this purse—and you will follow him. Adieu.

(She leaves. Night begins to come on.)

BURIDAN

Ah, indeed! This is a dream or a hoax.

PHILIPPE

What is it?

BURIDAN

This veiled woman.

PHILIPPE

Well?

BURIDAN

She's just said word-for-word to me—what a woman said to you.

PHILIPPE

A rendezvous?

BURIDAN

Like yours.

PHILIPPE

The time?

BURIDAN

The same as yours.

PHILIPPE

And a purse?

BURIDAN

Just like yours.

PHILIPPE

Let's see.

BURIDAN

Look at it.

PHILIPPE

This is magic! And are you going?

BURIDAN

I will go.

PHILIPPE

They must be sisters.

BURIDAN

So much the better. We will be brothers-in-law.

LANDRY

(at the door)

This way, master.

(Landry comes in with Gaultier D'Aulnay, then goes to Orsini's room.)

PHILIPPE

Hush, here's Gaultier. To me, brother, to me!

(He opens his arms.)

GAULTIER

Your hand, brother. Ah, here you are then. Is it really you?

PHILIPPE

It's me, yes.

GAULTIER

Do you still love me?

PHILIPPE

As the other half of myself.

GAULTIER

And you are right, brother. Hug me again. Who is this man?

PHILIPPE

A friend of a half hour, who did me a service which I will remember all my life. He got me out of the clutches of a dozen criminals, that I had thrown a curse and a goblet at, because they were speaking ill of you.

GAULTIER

(to Buridan)

Ah, thanks for him, thanks for me. If Gaultier D'Aulnay can be of use to you in some way, be he praying on the tomb of his mother or at his mistress' feet, he will rise and go to you and if you require his blood to save your life he will give it you as he gives you his hand.

BURIDAN

Gentlemen, it appears you love with a holy zeal.

PHILIPPE

Yes—you see, Captain, it's all we have left in the world he and I, for we are twins without relatives with a red cross on our left arms as the only sign of recognition—for we were exposed together nude on the steps of Notre Dame—we've been hungry and cold together—and we keep warm—satiated together.

GAULTIER

And, since that time, never apart for more than six months and when he dies, I will die, since he only came into the world a few hours before me and I must not survive him by more than a few hours—these things are written, believe it, and also between us, everything together, not alone—our horse, our purse, our sword on a sign, our life on a word. Goodbye, Captain—come to my place, brother.

PHILIPPE

Cannot, on my oath. I have to go somewhere where someone is waiting for me.

GAULTIER

Here only two hours and you have already got a rendezvous. Take care, brother!

(Two tavern boys pass by and close the windows.)

GAULTIER

For some time, the Seine has been full of cadavers; the grave has received many dead; but it is especially foreign gentlemen who are hooked to the shore—a bloody harvest! Take care, Captain, take care!

PHILIPPE

You hear, Captain, will you go?

BURIDAN

I will go.

PHILIPPE

And I, too.

GAULTIER

How long have you been here, Captain?

BURIDAN

For five days.

GAULTIER

(reflecting)

You, for two hours, him, for five days—you very young, he, also young. Don't go my friends—don't go.

PHILIPPE

We promised; promised on our honor.

GAULTIER

A promise is sacred. Go ahead, then, but tomorrow, tomorrow in the morning—brother.

PHILIPPE

Relax.

GAULTIER

(turning and taking the hand of Buridan)

When you wish, sire.

BURIDAN

Thanks.

(The clock bells ring for sunset.)

ORSINI

(entering)

Here's the lights out, gentlemen.

BURIDAN

(taking his cloak and leaving)

Adieu—they're waiting for me at the second tower of the Louvre.

PHILIPPE

Me, at the Rue Froid-Mantel.

GAULTIER

Me, at the palace.

(They leave.)

ORSINI

(alone)

(Closing the door and giving a little whistle, Landry and three men appear.)

ORSINI

And we, children, at the Tower of Nesle.

CURTAIN

ACT I
SCENE 2

Circular interior. Two doors to stage right, a window at the back with a balcony—chairs, etc.

Orsini, alone, leaning against the window.

One can hear thunder and see lightning.

ORSINI

Beautiful night for an orgy in the tower. Heaven is black, rain is falling, the city sleeps. A beautiful time for love; outside, thunder; inside, the touching of glasses and kisses and talk of love.

(loud laughter can be heard)

Laugh, young fools, laugh—me, I wait. You have an hour more to laugh and I, another hour to wait, as I waited yesterday, and as I will wait tomorrow. What an inexorable fate! Because their eyes have seen what they mustn't see, their eyes must be closed forever; because their lips have given and received kisses they ought not to receive or give, those lips must be shut, never to reopen as occurs except before the throne of God. But, still a misfortune well deserved by these impudent fools who rise to the first call of nocturnal love! Presumptuous idiots who think it's a simple thing to come by night, eyes blindfolded in this old tower to find three women to tell them "I love you" and drink wine—and exchange caresses with them.

A NIGHT WATCHMAN

(outside)

It is two o'clock, and all's well.

ORSINI

Two o'clock already!

(Landry enters.)

LANDRY

Master.

ORSINI

What do you want?

LANDRY

It's two o'clock—the watchman just passed.

ORSINI

Well—it is still a long time from dawn.

LANDRY

But the others are getting bored.

ORSINI

They are being paid.

LANDRY

Save your good pleasure, Master, but they are paid to strike not to wait. If it is going to be this way, they may double the price—for boredom rather than for killing.

ORSINI

Shut up—here's someone. Go away.

LANDRY

I am going; but what I said is no less true.

(Landry exits. Marguerite enters.)

MARGUERITE

Orsini!

ORSINI

Madame?

MARGUERITE

Where are your men?

ORSINI

There.

MARGUERITE

Ready?

ORSINI

All ready, Madame, all ready. The night is getting on.

MARGUERITE

Is it so late?

ORSINI

The storm is quieting.

MARGUERITE

Yes—listen to the thunder.

ORSINI

The day is coming.

MARGUERITE

You deceive yourself, Orsini, see how somber the night still is. Oh!

(She sits down.)

ORSINI

No matter, Madame—we must put out the candles, take up the cushions, close the flagons. Your boats are waiting for you. You must cross the Seine—return to your noble dwelling and leave us the masters here—the sole masters.

MARGUERITE

Oh—let me alone. This night doesn't resemble the preceding ones; this young man is not like the other young men—he resembles someone else—don't you think so, Orsini?

ORSINI

Who does he resemble, then?

MARGUERITE

He resembles my Gaultier D'Aulnay. I was shocked in looking at him to believe I was looking at my Gaultier—he's a child all of love and passion. He's a child who cannot be dangerous—right?

ORSINI

Oh, Madame, what are you saying? Think of it as a toy that must be used and broken—the more joy and abandonment you experience with that toy, the more it is to be feared. It is nearly three o'clock, Madame—retire—and leave the young men to us.

MARGUERITE

(rising)

Abandon him to you, Orsini? No way. He is mine. Go ask my sisters if they wish to give theirs up—if they choose to, fine, but as for mine, he must escape. Oh, I can do it, for all night I was careful, I kept on my mask—he hasn't seen me, Orsini, this noble young man—my face remains veiled to him. If he were to see me tomorrow he could not recognize me. Well, I will spare his life, I wish it thus. I will see him again safe and sound—let him be taken back to the town—let him live to recall this night, let him burn for the rest of his life with memories of love—for it will be one of those heavenly dreams one has only once on this earth. May it be for him as it will be for me.

ORSINI

It will be as you wish, Madame.

MARGUERITE

Yes, yes, save him—that's what I had to tell you, but hesitated to say to you. Now that I've told you, open the door, but put your daggers back in their scabbards; hasten—hurry.

(Orsini leaves.)

PHILIPPE

(outside)

But where are you, my life, where are you my love? Tell me your name—woman or angel, so I can call you by your name.

MARGUERITE

(as he enters)

Young man, here is the door.

PHILIPPE

What has this day done to me? Especially this night. There is neither day nor night. There are torches which burn, wines which sparkle, hearts which beat—and time which passes. Let's return.

MARGUERITE

No, no, we must separate.

PHILIPPE

Separate? Us? Oh! Who knows if I ever will find you again. I am yours as you are mine. To separate the rings on this chain is to break it.

MARGUERITE

Oh—you promised more moderation. Time is flying—my husband can awaken, look for me, here is the day!

PHILIPPE

No, no, it is not the day, it's the moon which glides between two clouds pushed on by the wind. Your old husband won't come yet. The old are confident and sleepy. One more hour, my beautiful mistress, an hour and then goodbye.

MARGUERITE

No, no, not an hour, not an instant. Leave—it is I who beg you, leave without looking behind you, without remembering this night of love—without speaking to anyone of it—without saying a word to your best friend. Leave—quit Paris, do you see, leave the city—I order you to do it—leave!

PHILIPPE

Well, yes, I am leaving, but your name? Tell me your name so that I can murmur it forever in my ear, so that it will engrave itself forever in my heart. Your name—so I can repeat it in my dreams. I can see that you are beautiful and noble. Your colors that I may wear them. I have found you because you wished it so—but for a long while I have sought you. Your name in one last kiss! and I am going.

MARGUERITE

I have no name for you! The night is over—all is finished between you and me. I am free and I set you free. We are finished with the hours spent together. I owe you nothing and you owe me nothing. Yet obey me if you love me. Obey me even if you don't love me, for I am a woman, and I am in my own home and I can command. Our nocturnal meeting is broken—I no longer know you. Leave.

PHILIPPE

Ah—that's the way it is. I beg and you rail at me—I supplicate and you run me off—well, I am going. Adieu, noble and honest woman who gives rendezvous in the night—to whom the shadows of the night are not enough and who needs to wear a mask—but I am not someone to be made a plaything for an hour. It won't be said that you can laugh at the role of dupe you've just made me play.

MARGUERITE

What do you want?

(Philippe tears a pin from Marguerite's headdress.)

PHILIPPE

Fear nothing, Madame, this will be less than nothing, a little mask by which I can recognize you, that's all.

(He scratches her face across her mask.)

MARGUERITE

Ah!

PHILIPPE

Now—tell me your name—or don't tell me. Take off your mask or put it on. I will recognize you.

MARGUERITE

You've wounded me, sir? This scratch is the same as if you saw my face. Fool, whom I wished to save, and who is going to die—! This mask, you see, this mask—pray to God. Let them remember only my first orders.

(She leaves.)

(Orsini has entered on the last remark and goes to the window, closes it and takes away the light. Complete night until the end of the act.)

(Buridan slowly comes out of the door at left, extends his arm—slides through the shadows and puts his hand on Philippe's arm.)

BURIDAN

Who is there?

PHILIPPE

Me?

BURIDAN

Who are you?

PHILIPPE

What's it matter to you?

BURIDAN

I know that voice.

(He pulls him to the window.)

PHILIPPE

Buridan.

BURIDAN

Philippe.

PHILIPPE

You here.

BURIDAN

Yes, God's blood, I am here—and I will wish to meet you elsewhere.

PHILIPPE

Why that?

BURIDAN

Don't you know where we are?

PHILIPPE

Where are we?

BURIDAN

You don't know who these women are?

PHILIPPE

You are very upset, Buridan.

BURIDAN

These women—don't you have some suspicion of their rank?

PHILIPPE

No.

BURIDAN

Haven't you noticed they must be great ladies? Their white hands, their cold smiles, their rich clothes, their soft voices, their false expressions. These are great ladies—you see! Grand ladies. Our story is the same isn't it? As soon as we arrived, they gave themselves to us—greeted us with a thousand caresses—to strangers—in the midst of this storm. They lost all restraint, they got drunk and let themselves be carried away, lost all modesty, forgot heaven and earth. Oh, these are great ladies, I repeat—very great ladies.

PHILIPPE

Well—?

BURIDAN

Well—doesn't that give you some fear?

PHILIPPE

Fear—what fear?

BURIDAN

The care they take to remain unknown.

PHILIPPE

Let me but see mine tomorrow and I will recognize her.

BURIDAN

Then she took off her mask?

PHILIPPE

No, but with this pin, I put a mark on her face she will wear a long while.

BURIDAN

Wretch! There was perhaps some hope of saving us, and you are killing us both.

PHILIPPE

How?

BURIDAN

(escorting him to the window)

Look before you.

PHILIPPE

The Louvre.

BURIDAN

At your feet.

PHILIPPE

The Seine.

BURIDAN

And around us, the Tower of Nesle.

PHILIPPE

The Tower of Nesle!

BURIDAN

Yes, yes, the old tower beneath which they are finding so many bodies.

PHILIPPE

And we are without arms! For they asked for your sword when you came in as they did mine?

BURIDAN

What use would they be? It's not a question of defending ourselves, it's a question of fleeing. Look at this door.

PHILIPPE

(trying the door)

Shut! Ah, listen—if I die, and if you live—you must avenge me.

BURIDAN

Yes, and if I die and you live, then vengeance is your job. You will go find your brother, Gaultier—your brother who can do anything—tell him—listen—it must be written—there must be proof.

PHILIPPE

Nor pen, nor ink, nor parchment.

BURIDAN

Here is a notebook. You still have this pen—on your arm, there are veins with blood on them—write so your brother will believe me—I am going to ask him vengeance for you—write—write—"I was murdered by"—I will put the name—for I know who—yes, I know and sign it. If you escape do for me what I would have done for you. Goodbye—let's each try to fly from our own side. Goodbye.

PHILIPPE

Goodbye comrade—for life—for death.

(They embrace—Philippe goes into the room from which he came—Buridan tries to go off and recoils before Landry who enters.

BURIDAN

Ah!

LANDRY

Say your prayers, my good sir.

BURIDAN

I know that voice.

LANDRY

My Captain.

BURIDAN

Landry! I must escape, my brave fellow—they want to assassinate me.

(Noise of a scream.)

BURIDAN

A scream—who was that?

LANDRY

It was your third companion—who was with the third sister—he's being strangled.

BURIDAN

You won't kill me, right?

LANDRY

I cannot save you, I would if I could.

BURIDAN

This stairway?

LANDRY

It is guarded.

BURIDAN

The window?

LANDRY

Can you swim?

BURIDAN

Yes—

LANDRY

(opening the window)

Then hurry—God protect you.

BURIDAN

(on the balcony)

Lord, Lord, have pity on me!

(He jumps—the noise of a body falling in the water can be heard.)

ORSINI

(entering)

Where is he?

LANDRY

In the River—it's done.

ORSINI

Was he quite dead?

LANDRY

Quite dead.

PHILIPPE

(comes in all bloody)

Help—help—brother, to me, my brother.

MARGUERITE

(entering, torch in hand)

"To see your face and then die," you said. Let it be as you wish—

(tearing off her mask)

Look and die!

PHILIPPE

Marguerite de Bourgogne! Queen of France.

(he dies)

WATCHMAN

(outside)

It is three o'clock and all's well.

CURTAIN

ACT II:
MARGUERITE DE BOURGOGNE
SCENE 3

Marguerite's apartment in the Louvre.

At rise, the Queen is lying on her bed. She awakes and calls one of her women.

MARGUERITE

Charlotte! Charlotte!

(Charlotte enters.)

MARGUERITE

Is it day, Charlotte?

CHARLOTTE

Yes, my lady—for a long while.

MARGUERITE

Draw the curtains slowly so the light doesn't hurt me. That's good. What is the weather like?

CHARLOTTE

(going to the window)

Beautiful. Last night's storm has swept the heavens of the least cloud—it's a blue cloth out there.

MARGUERITE

What's happening in the streets?

VEILED WOMAN

A young lord, wrapped in his cloak is talking before your windows with a Franciscan monk.

MARGUERITE

Do you know him?

CHARLOTTE

Yes, it's Milord Gaultier D'Aulnay.

MARGUERITE

Ah—doesn't he look about him?

CHARLOTTE

From time to time—he's left the monk and is coming in to the palace arcade.

MARGUERITE

(quickly)

Charlotte, go inquire after the health of my sisters Blanche and Jeanne. I will call you when I want news of them. You hear, I will call you.

CHARLOTTE

Yes, Madame.

MARGUERITE

He was there—waiting for me to awaken—and not daring to hasten it. Eyes fixed on my window—Gaultier, my handsome gentleman.

(Gaultier appearing from a little door screened by the bedstead.)

GAULTIER

Have all the angels of heaven showered over my Queen's bed to make her sleep peaceful and give her golden thoughts?

(He sits on the cushions of the platform.)

MARGUERITE

Yes, I had sweet thoughts, Gaultier, I dreamed of seeing a young man who resembled you—your eyes and your voice, your age—your transports of love—

GAULTIER

And this dream?

MARGUERITE

Let me recall—I've hardly awakened and my ideas are all confused—this dream had a terrible end, a sadness as if it had scratched my cheek.

GAULTIER

(seeing the scar)

Ah—in fact, Madame, you've been injured.

MARGUERITE

(recalling her ideas)

Yes, yes, I know it—a pin—a gold pin—a pin from my hair which rolled in my bed and has scratched me.

(aside)

Oh—I remember.

GAULTIER

Let's see—and why thus risk your beauty, my beloved Marguerite, your beauty is not yours—it is mine.

MARGUERITE

To whom were you speaking before my window?

GAULTIER

To a monk who was bringing me some notebooks on behalf of a stranger I saw yesterday who knew no one in Paris and who, fearing a misfortune would befall him in this great city, made me promise through his intermediary to open them if two days go by without my hearing from him—He's the Captain I met yesterday at Orsini's Tavern.

MARGUERITE

You will present your brother to me this morning; I love him already from the love I have for you.

GAULTIER

Oh, my beautiful queen. Keep your love intact for me—for I would be jealous—even of my brother. Yes—he will come this morning to your lover—he's a fine and loyal young man, Marguerite—he's half of my life; he's my second soul.

MARGUERITE

And the first?

GAULTIER

You are the first or rather you are everything for me, your soul, life, existence; I live in you. And I count the beats of my heart when I put my hand in yours. Oh! If you loved me as I love you, Marguerite, you would be all for me, as I am all for you.

MARGUERITE

No, my friend, no. Leave me a pure love—if I were to give in to you today, perhaps, tomorrow I would fear you. An indiscretion, a word is mortal for a Queen. Be content to love me, Gaultier, and to know how I love to listen to you.

GAULTIER

Perhaps it is because the King is returning tomorrow, alas!

MARGUERITE

Tomorrow—and with him, goodbye to our liberty—goodbye to our lengthy and sweet conversations. Oh, let us speak of something else. Does this scar show up too much?

GAULTIER

Yes.

MARGUERITE

What do I hear in that room to the side?

GAULTIER

(rising)

The noise made by our young lords waiting for the lover of the Queen.

MARGUERITE

We mustn't make them wait; they perhaps will wonder if I have forgotten them. I will find you again in the midst of them, right? My Lord, my true Lord, and master who would be the only one if it was love that made royalty—au revoir.

GAULTIER

Already?

MARGUERITE

It must be—go!

(She draws a cord that hangs close. Gaultier is in the room. Marguerite's arm strikes out between the curtains. Gaultier kisses her hand.)

MARGUERITE

Charlotte! Charlotte! Charlotte!

CHARLOTTE

(behind the curtain)

Madame?

MARGUERITE

(withdrawing her hand)

Open the apartment.

(Savoisy, Pierrefonds and Raoul with courtiers enter.)

SAVOISY

Ah! Good. Afternoon is ahead of us. It's proper. How is the Marguerite of all Marguerites, Queen of France, Navarre and Bourgogne this morning?

GAULTIER

I don't know gentlemen, I just got here. I hoped to see my brother in your midst. Greetings, gentlemen, greetings! What news this morning?

PIERREFONDS

Nothing very new. The King will be here tomorrow; he will have a beautiful entry to his good city. The orders are given by Lord de Marigny that the good citizens rejoice and cry "Noel" on his way—while waiting he will cry "Curse" on the banks of the Seine.

GAULTIER

And why?

SAVOISY

The stream has just cast another drowned body on his river; and the people catch strange fish.

PIERREFONDS

These are curses which will fall back on this damned Marigny who is charged with the safety of the city. My word, the dead will be welcome if we could suffocate the prime minister under a pile of cadavers.

GAULTIER

(going to courtiers)

Strange things are happening—have none of you seen my brother, gentlemen?

PIERREFONDS

If the King is not careful, Milords, he will lose a third of his population in the water—the noblest and richest. What devilish vertigo pushes our young men to such an end, good only for kittens and low life?

SAVOISY

Oh—Milords, are you going to believe that those who leave the Seine dead entered the water voluntarily while living? No way.

PIERREFONDS

At least, if they weren't led there by demons and wanton flames. I don't see too much.

SAVOISY

The River is indiscreet and doesn't keep the secrets confided to it. One would rather dig a tomb in the water than on land, except the water rejects and the Earth protects from the Hotel Saint Paul right up to the Louvre. There are many houses that bathe their feet in the water and many windows in these houses.

RAOUL

The Lord de Savoisy is right and the Tower of Nesle for his Count.

SAVOISY

Yes, I went by the Louvre at two in the morning and the Tower of Nesle was brilliantly lit. Torches all over the place. It was a feast night at the Tower. I don't like that great mass of stone which seems at night an evil genius watching the city—its great mass immobile, hurling at intervals fire from all its openings like a hole from Hell—silent under the black heaven with the river heaving at its feet. If you know what the people say—

GAULTIER

Gentlemen, you forget it is a royal hotel.

SAVOISY

Anyway, the King is coming tomorrow, and the King, you know, gentlemen, doesn't like news he doesn't make himself. Right, Monsieur de Marigny?

(Marigny entering.)

MARIGNY

What were you talking about, gentlemen? Then I can reply to your question.

SAVOISY

We were saying that the people of Paris were a lucky people to have Louis X for King and M. de Marigny for Prime Minister.

MARIGNY

And at least half of this joy won't last long, if it were up to you, Monsieur de Savoisy.

A PAGE

(announcing)

The Queen, Milords.

(The curtains draw back.)

MARGUERITE

God protect you, Milords. You know that the King, my lord and master, arrives tomorrow—thus if you have some bounty to ask of the Regent, hurry, for I have only one more day of power.

SAVOISY

We won't lose you, Madame, you will always be our Queen—Queen by blood, Queen by beauty, and you will always be the true Regent of France—as for the king, may God protect him! Let us preserve his eyes and heart.

MARGUERITE

You flatter me, count. Good day, Lord Gaultier—you were to present your brother to me.

GAULTIER

And you see me very uneasy about him, Madame. Oh, the cursed city of Paris is full of gypsies and sorcerers. Don't shrug your shoulders, Monsieur de Marigny, I am not accusing you. The city is always growing and this escapes your surveillance. This very morning, they found on the river a little below the Tower of Nesle—a body.

MARIGNY

Two, sir.

MARGUERITE

(aside)

Two!

GAULTIER

And who would commit these murders if not gypsies and sorcerers who need blood for their conjuring. Do you believe you can force nature to reveal its secrets without horrible profanations?

MARGUERITE

You forget, Milord Gaultier, that Monsieur de Marigny doesn't believe in sorcery.

SAVOISY

(by the window)

He doesn't believe it? Eh, Madame, one has only to close one's eyes on the street to see necromancers and sorcerers—right before your palace, and here's one who seems to wait for a consultation, so he has fixed his eyes furiously—on your window.

MARGUERITE

Call him, Lord de Savoisy—I wouldn't be angry if he foretold what will happen to Monsieur de Marigny on the return of the King. Would you like it, gentlemen?

PIERREFONDS

Our Queen is mistress.

SAVOISY

(crying out the window)

Come here, Gypsy—and give us good news—it is a Queen who wishes to know the future.

MARGUERITE

Come gentlemen—we must receive this wise necromancer with dignity.

SAVOISY

Yes, without doubt, but his knowledge can come to him equally from God or from Satan—let us make the sign of the cross, just in case.

(They all cross themselves with the exception of Marigny.)

SAVOISY

Here he comes, by God. He's walked through the walls.

(going to him)

Cursed Gypsy—the Queen made you come to speak of the Prime Minister.

GYPSY

(entering at the door to the right)

Let me go to her, if you want me to speak to her. Enguerrand de Marigny—I am here.

MARIGNY

Listen, sorcerer, if you want to be welcome here, announce a thousand disgraces for me rather than one; a thousand deaths rather than one death and then add still more your predictions which the others will find joyous and confiding, while you will find me at ease and incredulous.

GYPSY

Enguerrand, I have only one disgrace and one death to you—but your disgrace is near and your death will be terrible. If you have some score to settle with God, hasten, for, by my voice, he gives you only three days.

MARIGNY

Thanks, Gypsy—for none of us knows if he has even three hours, the others are waiting for you. Thanks.

GYPSY

What do you want me to tell you, Gaultier D'Aulnay? At your age, this is yesterday; the future is tomorrow.

GAULTIER

Well, speak to me of the present.

GYPSY

Child, rather ask of the past, or rather ask me of the future—the present—no—no!

GAULTIER

Sorcerer, I want to know it? What's happening now to me?

GYPSY

You are waiting for your brother and your brother doesn't come.

GAULTIER

And my brother—where is he?

GYPSY

The people are crowded around him on the banks of the Seine.

GAULTIER

My brother?

GYPSY

They surround two bodies crying "Misfortune."

GAULTIER

My brother?

GYPSY

Come down and run to the grave.

GAULTIER

My brother.

GYPSY

And while you're there, look at the left arm of the drowned man and with one voice cry, "Misfortune, Misfortune."

GAULTIER

(rushing out)

My brother! My brother!

GYPSY

(turning to the Queen)

And you, Marguerite de Bourgogne, don't you want to know something? Or do you imagine I have nothing to tell you? Do you think that a royal destiny is superhuman and that mortal eyes cannot read it?

MARGUERITE

I don't wish to know anything.

GYPSY

And you had me come, now here I am, Marguerite—now you must listen to me.

MARGUERITE

(alone on her throne)

Don't wander off, Monsieur de Marigny.

GYPSY

O Marguerite, Marguerite, whose nights outside are dark and well lit within.

MARGUERITE

What's the name of this Gypsy; what's his name—what's he want from me?

GYPSY

(putting his foot on the first step of the throne)

Marguerite, is there one cadaver missing from your account? Didn't you expect to hear of three rather than two?

MARGUERITE

(rising)

Shut up—or tell me: who gives you this power of divination?

GYPSY

(showing her the gold pin from her headdress)

Here's my talisman, Marguerite. Ah, you put your hand to your cheek. Fine, all is said.

(aside)

It is she.

(aloud)

I must tell you one last word and no one must hear. Stand off, Lord de Marigny.

MARIGNY

Gypsy, I take my orders only from the Queen.

MARGUERITE

(coming down)

Stand off—stand off.

GYPSY

You see I know everything, Marguerite, your love, your honor, your life are in my hands. Marguerite, this evening, after curfew, I will be waiting for you at Orsini's Tavern. I must speak to you alone.

MARGUERITE

Can a Queen of France leave alone at that hour?

GYPSY

It's no further from here to the Gate of Saint Honoré than to the Tower of Nesle.

MARGUERITE

I will go, I will go.

GYPSY

You will bring a parchment and the state seal.

MARGUERITE

So be it! But until then?

GAULTIER

Until then, you are going back into your apartment which will be closed to everyone.

MARGUERITE

To everyone?

GYPSY

Even to Gaultier D'Aulnay, especially to Gaultier D'Aulnay—Milords, the Queen thanks you and prays God to protect you—forbid entrance to your apartments.

MARGUERITE

Guards—allow no one to enter.

GYPSY

Till this evening at Orsini's, Marguerite.

MARGUERITE

(leaving)

Till this evening.

(The Gypsy goes amidst the lords who make way for him and look at him with terror.)

SAVOISY

Milords, can you imagine such a thing? Isn't this man Satan?

PIERREFONDS

What could he have said to the Queen?

SAVOISY

Monsieur de Marigny, you were near Marguerite—did you hear his prediction?

MARIGNY

It's possible, gentlemen, but I don't remember what he said to me.

SAVOISY

Well—from now on will you believe in sorcerers?

MARIGNY

Why more than before? He predicted my disgrace; I am still minister; he predicted my death—true—God! Gentlemen, if one of you is tempted to assure yourself that I am still living, he need only speak. I have a sword at my side which will take care in such a case to reply for its master.

GAULTIER

(rushes into the hall)

Justice! Justice!

ALL

Gaultier.

GAULTIER

Milords—it was my brother, my brother Philippe, my only friend, my only relative! My brother strangled, drowned—my brother on the river bank! Curse, I want justice. I want his murderer, so I can strangle him, so I can trample him under my feet. His assassin, Savoisy, do you know who it is?

SAVOISY

But you are out of your head.

GAULTIER

No, I am cursed. My rank, my blood, my gold to whoever will tell me. Monsieur de Marigny, be careful—it is you who reply to me; you are the guardian of the city—of Paris, not a drop of blood is spilled without you knowing. Where is the Queen? I wish to see the Queen. I wish to see Marguerite. Marguerite will do me justice. My brother—my brother.

(He hurls himself towards the door in the rear.)

SAVOISY

Gaultier, my friend.

GAULTIER

I have no friend, I had only a brother—he must live or his murderer die! Marguerite! Marguerite!

(he shakes the door)

It is I. It is I. Open!

A CAPTAIN

No one can pass.

GAULTIER

I, I, I can pass—let me—Marguerite—my brother.

(The guards grab him by the arms and pull him away. He draws his sword.)

GAULTIER

I must see her. I wish it.

(The guards disarm him. He falls and rolls on the floor.)

GAULTIER

Ah, curse! Ah, my brother, my brother!

CURTAIN

ACT II
SCENE 4

Orsini's Tavern. Same as first act.

ORSINI

(alone)

It seems there's nothing to do tonight at the tower. Better that way. For, some day all this spilling of blood will fall back on someone, and misfortune to whoever is designated by God to expiate.

(a knocking, he rises)

Have I spoken too soon?

(another knock)

Who goes there?

MARGUERITE

(outside)

Open, it is I!

ORSINI

The Queen.

(opening)

Alone at this hour?

MARGUERITE

(sitting)

Yes, alone and at this hour! It's strange, isn't it? And what has happened to me is strange, too. Listen, didn't someone knock?

ORSINI

No.

MARGUERITE

You've got to give me this room for a half hour.

ORSINI

The house and the master are yours—dispose of them.

(A knocking.)

MARGUERITE

(rising)

This time someone knocks.

ORSINI

Do you want me to open?

MARGUERITE

It's my concern. Let me alone.

ORSINI

If the Queen has need of me, her servant will be there.

MARGUERITE

That's fine. Let the servant remember only that he must hear nothing!

ORSINI

He will be stupid, as if he were mute.

(He leaves—the knocking starts again.)

MARGUERITE

Is it you?

BURIDAN

Is it me?

MARGUERITE

(opening and recoiling)

This is not the gypsy.

BURIDAN

No—it's the captain—but if the captain is the gypsy, he's back all the same, right? I prefer this costume; it's more defensible if need be, than this morning's costume. The time's short at this hour of night, the streets are bad. Anyway, right or wrong it's a precaution I believed I needed to take.

MARGUERITE

You see I have come.

BURIDAN

And you have done well, Queen.

MARGUERITE

You recognize that on my part at least it's an act of compliance.

BURIDAN

Whether you came from compliance or from fear, I was sure of finding you here—for me that was essential.

MARGUERITE

You are not from Bohemia?

BURIDAN

No, by the grace of God; I am a Christian or rather I was, but for a long time I've lost my faith, having no more hope. Let's speak of something else.

(He takes a chain.)

MARGUERITE

I am used to men speaking to me, standing with hats off.

BURIDAN

I will speak to you standing and hat off, Marguerite, because you are a woman—not because you are a Queen. Look around us. Is there a single object, a single object that can recognize the rank you boast of, foolish one? These black and smoke darkened walls hardly resemble the apartments of a Queen? Is this smoky lamp, this half-broken table furniture for a Queen? Queen—where are your guards? Queen—where is your throne? Here there is only a man and a woman, and since the man is easy and the woman trembles, the man is the King.

MARGUERITE

But who brings me here to speak to me this way? Where are you from that you think I am in your power—and what makes you believe that I tremble?

BURIDAN

Who am I? Right now I am Captain Buridan. Perhaps I have another name which would be better known to you. For the moment, there is no need for you to know it. From where do I think you are in my power—well, if you hadn't thought so yourself you wouldn't come thus. What makes me think you tremble—it's that by your count and mine, a body is necessary that the Seine has rejected and could reject only two last night.

MARGUERITE

And the third?

BURIDAN

The third? The third exists, Marguerite; the third is Buridan, the Captain, the man who is before you.

MARGUERITE

(rising)

It's impossible.

BURIDAN

Impossible! Listen, Marguerite, do you want me to tell you what happened last night at the Tower?

MARGUERITE

Speak.

BURIDAN

There were three women; the Princess Jeanne, the Princess Blanche, and the Queen Marguerite. There were three men—Hector de Chevreuse, Buridan the Captain, and Philippe D'Aulnay.

MARGUERITE

Philippe D'Aulnay?

BURIDAN

Yes, Philippe D'Aulnay, the brother of Gaultier—he's the one who wanted to see under your mask; he's the one who made the scratch on your face.

MARGUERITE

Well, Hector and Philippe are dead—and you are the sole survivor? Right?

BURIDAN

The sole.

MARGUERITE

And you told yourself, "I will reveal what happened and I will betray the Queen; the Queen loves Gaultier D'Aulnay and I will tell Gaultier that she killed his brother." You are mad, Buridan, for no one will believe you. You are indeed bold, for now I know your secret as you know mine—I can call—make a sign and in five minutes, Buridan, the Captain will have rejoined Hector de Chevreuse and Philippe D'Aulnay.

BURIDAN

Do it—and Gaultier D'Aulnay will open a notebook that he has received from a Franciscan monk that he has sworn to open if he does not hear from me and see me. If you kill me, Marguerite, he won't see me and he will open the notebook.

MARGUERITE

Do you think he believes your writing more than your words?

BURIDAN

No, Marguerite, no; but he will believe the writing of his brother, his brother's last words, written in his own blood, signed by his own hand. "I was murdered by Marguerite de Bourgogne." You left Philippe only for a moment—unwise, it was long enough.

It will take more than killing me to get rid of me. Put twenty knives in my heart and you won't find my secret. Send me to join my companions of last night in the Seine and my secret will float up out of the Seine—Gaultier will be my avenger—he will come to ask you to account for the death of his brother and mine. Well—am I a madman or a fool, or are my measures well taken?

MARGUERITE

If things are really this way—

BURIDAN

They are—

MARGUERITE

What do you want from me then? Do you want money? You want to fill your hands with treasure? Is the death of an enemy necessary to you? Here is the seal and the parchment you had me bring. Are you ambitious? I can make you whatever you desire in the state. Speak, what do you want?

BURIDAN

I want all that.

(sitting)

Listen to me, Marguerite, as I told you, here there is neither King nor Queen—only a man and a woman who are going to make a contract. And disaster to whichever of the two breaks it before being assured of the other's death. Marguerite, I want enough gold to pave a palace.

MARGUERITE

You shall have it, if I have to melt the scepter and crown.

BURIDAN

I want to be Prime Minister.

MARGUERITE

The Lord Enguerrand de Marigny holds that position.

BURIDAN

I want his title and his place.

MARGUERITE

But you cannot have it without his death.

BURIDAN

I want his title and his place.

MARGUERITE

You shall have them.

BURIDAN

And I will allow your lover and I will protect your secret. That's fine.

(rising)

To the two of us now, to the two of us, the realm of France—to the two of us—we will rebuild the state with a signature. The two of us will be the true King and I will keep quiet, Marguerite, and you will have your barge on the river each night; and I will wall up the windows of the Louvre which face the Tower of Nesle. Do you accept Marguerite?

MARGUERITE

I accept.

BURIDAN

You understand, Marguerite, tomorrow at this hour, I wish to be Prime Minister.

MARGUERITE

You will be.

BURIDAN

And tomorrow morning I will go to court to retrieve my notebook.

MARGUERITE

(rising)

You will be well received.

BURIDAN

(taking a parchment and giving it to her to sign)

The order to arrest Enguerrand de Marigny.

MARGUERITE

(signing)

Here it is.

BURIDAN

All is well. Adieu, Marguerite, until tomorrow.

(He takes his cloak and leaves.)

MARGUERITE

(alone)

Until tomorrow, demon! Oh! If I ever one day hold you in my hands as you hold me in yours tonight! If that cursed notebook—. Wretch, wretch, for you to come to me like this and threaten me—me, daughter of a Duke, wife of a King—regent of France. Me! Oh—this notebook—half of my blood to whoever will give them to me. If I could see Gaultier before tomorrow, if I could get the notebook away from him!

Gaultier, who will only speak to me of his brother, who is going to ask justice from me for the murder of his brother—but he loves me more than anything else in the world—and if he fears losing me, he will forget everything—even his brother. I've got to see him this evening. Where can I find him? I tremble to confide myself farther to this Italian—he already knows too many of my secrets! It seems to me I saw the door open—Buridan didn't close it—it's opening—a man—Orsini! To me, Orsini!

GAULTIER

(entering)

Marguerite! It's you, Marguerite!

MARGUERITE

Gaultier!

(aside)

My good angel has sent him to me.

GAULTIER

I have been looking for you the whole day to demand justice from you, Marguerite—I came to Orsini's for him to tell me if he knows anything about my brother's death. For I must have justice. And here you are my Queen! Justice! Justice!

MARGUERITE

And I, I came to Orsini counting to find you here, for before separating myself from you, I wanted to say goodbye.

GAULTIER

Goodbye, you say—Pardon, I don't understand very well—for a single idea pursues me, obsesses me—I am always seeing the drowned body of my brother, pierced with stab wounds and soaking wet—I've got to have his murderer, Marguerite.

MARGUERITE

Yes, I have given orders—your brother will be avenged, Gaultier—we will find his murderer, I swear it to you, but the King is arriving tomorrow and we must separate.

GAULTIER

Us, separate? What are you saying that for? My thoughts are like a stormy night and what you just said to me is like a flash of light which allows me to read for a moment. Yes—we will separate—yes, when my brother has been avenged.

MARGUERITE

No—we will separate tomorrow. The King is returning tomorrow. Oh, why, in the heart of my Gaultier is the heart which was entirely his Marguerite's—another emotion has come to replace love? Even yesterday, it was all mine, this heart—

(she puts her hands on his breast)

(aside)

The notebook is there.

GAULTIER

Yes, entirely given over to vengeance, then, afterwards—entirely yours.

MARGUERITE

What's this here?

GAULTIER

It's a notebook.

MARGUERITE

Yes, a notebook given to you by some monk—you are the happy

repository of thoughts of some woman of my court?

GAULTIER

Oh, Marguerite! Are you jesting with me? No, this notebook comes to me from a captain I met but once—whose name I don't even know—and who sent them to me, I don't know why and, who was here yesterday, with my brother—my poor brother.

MARGUERITE

You think I will believe that Gaultier? But never mind! Jealousy does not belong to those who are separating forever—? Goodbye, Gaultier, goodbye.

GAULTIER

What are you doing, Marguerite? Are you trying to make me go mad? I came to you in despair, to speak to you of my brother, and you speak to me of leaving—a great misfortune consumes me and you overwhelm me with a second! Why part? Why tell me goodbye?

MARGUERITE

The King has his suspicions, Gaultier, he mustn't find you here—besides, you will take the notebook with you to comfort you—

GAULTIER

You really believe that it is from a woman?

MARGUERITE

I am sure of it, if not, you would have shown it to me a thousand times by now.

GAULTIER

But can I? Are they mine? I have sworn on my honor not to open it but to return them to whom they belong if he reclaims them from me—can I make something clearer when I don't understand it myself? I have sworn on my honor that they won't leave my hands. That's all. I have sworn.

MARGUERITE

And I, haven't I sworn on honor I have violated no oath for you? Do you forget that I have been perjured for you—for the perjury is in loving rather than in adultery? Forget and keep your word, and I, I will keep my jealousy.

GAULTIER

Marguerite, in the name of heaven—!

MARGUERITE

The honor! The honor of a man! And is the honor of a woman nothing then? You have sworn. But as for me, a word, a single thought of you, has made me forget my oath to God, and I will forget it again, and if you ask it of me, I will forget the entire world for you.

GAULTIER

And yet, you wish that I leave! You want us to separate.

MARGUERITE

Yes, yes, I have promised this separation to the holy tribunal.

Well, if you exact it, if I was positive the notebook was not from a woman, well, I would brave the curse of God as I brave that of men for consider that at the court they laugh at the purity of our love! They are sure I'm guilty, aren't they? As if I really were; well, despite the necessity of your departure if you begged me, as I beg you, "Stay, my Gaultier, stay—let my reputation, my power be murdered but stay—stay near me, near me forever."

GAULTIER

You would do it?

MARGUERITE

Yes, but I am a woman, for whom honor is nothing, who can perjure herself with impunity and can be tortured at leisure, since she doesn't have the word of a gentleman; who can die of jealousy since someone keeps his oath.

GAULTIER

But if one ever knew—

MARGUERITE

Who will know it? Do we have witnesses here?

GAULTIER

You will return it to me before ten o'clock tomorrow.

MARGUERITE

I will give it back to you right away.

GAULTIER

May God forgive me! Is it any angel or a demon who makes me forget my brother, my oaths, my honor?

MARGUERITE

(taking the notebook in her hand)

I have it.

(She goes to the lamp and looks quickly at the notebook and tears out some pages.)

GAULTIER

Oh, Marguerite! Marguerite! Oh, human weakness—oh, pardon my brother—! Did I come to speak of love? Did I come to reassure the frivolous fears of a woman? I came to avenge you, my brother, forgive me.

MARGUERITE

(returning to him)

Oh, I was foolish! No, no, there was nothing in this notebook; it wasn't a woman who gave them to you. My Gaultier didn't lie when he said he loved me; that he loved only me! Well, me too, I love only him. I, too, will keep my promise and we will not be separated, little matter the King's suspicions; I will be so happy to suffer for my knight.

GAULTIER

Let's think about my brother, Marguerite.

MARGUERITE

Well, my friend, some research has already been done and they suspect—

GAULTIER

Who do they suspect?

MARGUERITE

A foreign Captain who has only been here a few days and who must appear at court tomorrow for the first time.

GAULTIER

His name?

MARGUERITE

Buridan, I believe.

GAULTIER

Buridan! And you have already given the order for his arrest, right?

MARGUERITE

I just learned of it and I haven't given the order yet, Captain of my guards.

GAULTIER

The order, the order! Let me arrest this man myself. Oh— no other shall arrest the murderer of my brother. The order,

Marguerite! The order in the name of heaven!

MARGUERITE

You will arrest him yourself?

GAULTIER

Yes, were he praying at the foot of the altar, I would tear him from it; yes, I will arrest him wherever he is.

MARGUERITE

(going to a table and signing a parchment)

Here is the order.

GAULTIER

Thanks! Thanks! my Queen.

MARGUERITE

(aside, threatening)

Oh! Buridan, now I hold your life in my hands.

CURTAIN

ACT III: ENGUERRAND DE MARIGNY
SCENE 5

Before the old Louvre. At the left, the front of the palace. With an accessible balcony and a postern gate.

At the rise of the curtain, Richard is watching the river flow by—other roughs talk and look at the Louvre.

SIMON

Fine! It's you, master Richard. From scavenger you've turned fisherman?

RICHARD

No, but you know all the nobility of the realm are going to the devil. And as it appears the way is shorter by water than by land, they're taking to the water.

SIMON

What are you doing there, nose to the river, backside to the Louvre?

RICHARD

I am looking to the base of the old Tower of Nesle to see if some nobleman's cape is passing; then to carry—bon voyage.

GUARDSMAN

(at the postern gate)

Hola—you scum—go talk further off.

RICHARD

Thanks, Mr. Guardsman.

(going)

May the devil twist your neck in your pepper box.

(Savoisy enters, followed by a page.)

SAVOISY

(finding himself face to face with Richard)

Take the lower steps, Clown!

RICHARD

(going down)

Yes, my Lord.

(going)

You will be at the height of the Seine, some day.

SAVOISY

You are saying something, I believe?

RICHARD

I am praying God to protect you as you deserve.

SAVOISY

Thanks a lot.

PAGE

The door of the Louvre is shut, Milord.

SAVOISY

This cannot be, Olivier; it is nine o'clock.

PAGE

See for yourself.

SAVOISY

There's something strange.

(to another Lord who follows with his page)

Raoul, do you understand what's happened?

RAOUL

What is going on?

SAVOISY

The Louvre is closed at this time?

RAOUL

Let's wait a moment. They are going to open without a doubt.

SAVOISY

The weather is fine! Let's walk about while we wait.

RAOUL

Guardsman!

GUARDSMAN

Milord?

RAOUL

Do you know why this door isn't open?

GUARDSMAN

No, Milord.

PIERREFONDS

(arriving)

Greetings, gentlemen. It appears that the Queen is going to hold her court this morning from her balcony.

SAVOISY

You have got it right from the first, Lord de Pierrefonds.

(Buridan enters with five guards.)

BURIDAN

(to a guard)

Stay here.

SAVOISY

Since you are such an excellent sorcerer, can you tell me who is this newcomer; and is he a marquis or duke, to have a five man guard?

PIERREFONDS

I don't know him. Without doubt he's some Italian fortune-hunter.

SAVOISY

And who's behind what he takes.

BURIDAN

(stopping and looking at them)

What is necessary to keep what he shall take is at his side, Milords.

SAVOISY

Then you will give me your secret, my master?

BURIDAN

I hope I won't have to teach you a lesson for you to learn it.

SAVOISY

It seems to me I have already heard this voice.

RAOUL and PIERREFONDS

Me, too.

SAVOISY

Ah! Here is our worthy minister, Lord Enguerrand de Marigny, who is going to mount his guard with us.

BURIDAN

(to his guards)

Attention.

(Marigny tries to enter the Louvre.)

MARIGNY

Where are you coming from that no one can enter the palace?

BURIDAN

I am going to tell you; it's because there was an arrest to make this morning and the interior of the palace is like an asylum.

MARIGNY

An arrest without my knowing of it?

BURIDAN

I was waiting for you here my lord, to instruct you—read.

SAVOISY

(to the other lords who watch astonished)

It seems to me that things are getting complicated.

MARIGNY

Give it here.

BURIDAN

Read aloud.

MARIGNY

"Order of Marguerite de Bourgogne, Queen Regent of France, to Captain Buridan, to arrest and seize the person wherever he may find him of the Lord, Enguerrand de Marigny."

BURIDAN

I am the Captain Buridan.

MARIGNY

You are arresting me by order of the Queen?

BURIDAN

Your sword!

MARIGNY

Here it is—draw it from its scabbard, sir. It is pure and without stains, isn't it? And how the execution will draw my soul from its body—it will be like this sword.

(Marguerite and Gaultier appear on the balcony.)

GAULTIER

Is he among these young lords, Marguerite?

MARGUERITE

He is the one who is speaking to Marigny, and who holds the naked sword.

GAULTIER

Fine.

(They both disappear.)

MARIGNY

I am ready, let's go.

BURIDAN

(to the guards)

Conduct the Lord Enguerrand de Marigny to the Château de Vincennes.

MARIGNY

And from there?

BURIDAN

To Montfaucon probably, Milord; you have taken care to raise the gibbet—it is proper for you to try it. You won't complain.

MARIGNY

Captain, I built it for criminals and not martyrs. Let God's will be done!

SAVOISY

Well, I reply that, if he escapes, the minister will believe in sorcerers from now on.

BURIDAN

(letting his head fall on his breast)

This man is upright.

PIERREFONDS

Ah! Miracle! The postern gate is opening, gentlemen.

SAVOISY

To let someone leave, it seems to me, but not to allow us to enter.

(Gaultier with four guards puts his hand on Buridan's shoulders, whose back is turned to him.)

SAVOISY

Are you Captain Buridan?

BURIDAN

(turning)

I am.

GAULTIER

What! It is you, you who were at the Orsini Tavern with my brother—you are Buridan, the one suspected and accused of his murder.

BURIDAN

(watching the balcony)

Ah—I am accused?

GAULTIER

In reality, it was you who invented this funereal rendezvous. I advised him against it. You drew him on, poor Philippe—it is indeed you! Read this order of the Queen, sir.

SAVOISY

Well, well—has the Queen spent the night signing orders?

GAULTIER

Read aloud.

BURIDAN

"Order of Marguerite de Bourgogne, Queen Regent of France to Captain Gaultier D'Aulnay to seize the person of Captain Buridan wherever he may be found." And you are chosen to arrest me?

GAULTIER

Your sword!

BURIDAN

Here it is. My notebook.

GAULTIER

Your notebook.

BURIDAN

Yes, don't you have it anymore?

SAVOISY

Good—it looks like they're arresting everybody today.

(Buridan receives the notebook from Gaultier—and looks

quickly.)

BURIDAN

Curses! Gaultier! Gaultier. This notebook left your hands?

GAULTIER

What are you saying?

BURIDAN

This notebook went from your hands to the Queen's?

GAULTIER

What are you talking about?

BURIDAN

One moment, one moment—right? By force or surprise—this notebook left your hands for a minute? Admit it!

GAULTIER

I admit it. Well?

BURIDAN

Well—in that instant, short as it may have been—it suffices for an arrest and a death—this arrest is mine—and it will recoil on you, for it is you who are killing me.

GAULTIER

Me?

BURIDAN

You see where someone has torn out a page?

GAULTIER

Yes.

BURIDAN

Yes—well this missing page was written by your brother—in his blood; signed by his hand.

GAULTIER

It was what? Finish?

BURIDAN

Oh! You won't believe it now, now that the page is torn for you are blind—for you are a fool.

GAULTIER

What was there? In the name of heaven—what was written on that page?

BURIDAN

It was there written—

MARGUERITE

(appearing on the balcony)

Guards, escort this man to the prison of the Grand Chalet.

(The guards surround Buridan.)

GAULTIER

But what was there?

BURIDAN

It said, "Gaultier D'Aulnay is a man without faith and without honor—who cannot keep for one day what was confided to his honor and faith." That's what was written there, disloyal gentleman. Well played, Marguerite—to you the first round, but to me the revenge, I hope! Let's go, gentlemen.

(They leave.)

SAVOISY

If I understand any of this, let Satan carry me off.

MARGUERITE

You forget that the door of the Louvre is open, Milord, and that the Queen is waiting on you!

SAVOISY

Ah, that's true! Let us go pay our court to the Queen.

CURTAIN

ACT III
SCENE 6

A cell in the Chalet.

Buridan is alone, lying prone, chained.

BURIDAN

One of the men who brought me here, shook my hand—but what can he do for me—supposing even that I am not deceived? Bring me some fresh water, some bread not quite so black—and a priest at the hour of my execution?

I counted two hundred and twenty steps we went down and a dozen doors opened.

Come, Buridan, come, think of putting your conscience in order—you've a long and complicated account to settle with Satan. Fool! Ten times fool I have been! I knew men break their honor like glass which falls like snow, when the breath of an ardent, woman blows on it and I suspended my life on such a thread. Fool! A hundred, a thousand times, fool! How happy she is now, how she jests—how she draws her lover into her arms—as each of her kisses tears remorse from Gaultier's heart. As for me, I—I roll on the ground of my cell. I ought to have separated from the young man—if ever—

(laughing)

It's possible—it's the only star in a dark sky. It's a small, weak light, for a lost voyager. She will want to see me—to insult me at my death. O demons! Demons who inhabit the hearts of women. Oh—I hope you haven't forgotten to install the perverse sentiment I believe is there, for it is on them that I am counting. But who can the man be who shook my hand, while bringing me here? Perhaps I am going to know, for the door is opening.

LANDRY

(entering)

Captain—where are you?

BURIDAN

Here.

LANDRY

It's me.

BURIDAN

Who, you? I can't see.

LANDRY

Must you see your friends to recognize them?

BURIDAN

That was Landry's voice.

LANDRY

Right.

BURIDAN

Can you save me?

LANDRY

Impossible.

BURIDAN

What the devil are you coming here for?

LANDRY

I've been a jailor since yesterday.

BURIDAN

It appears you are getting titles—jailor at the Chalet, assassin at the Tower of Nesle! Marguerite de Bourgogne must give you plenty of work in these two jobs.

LANDRY

Indeed, yes.

BURIDAN

And you cannot do anything for me here—not even bring me a confessor that I designate?

LANDRY

No, but I can listen to your confession so as to repeat it word for word to a priest and if there is a penitence, word of a soldier, I will perform it for you.

BURIDAN

Imbecile! Can you get me something to write on?

LANDRY

Impossible.

BURIDAN

Can you feel in my pocket and take a purse full of gold?

LANDRY

Yes, Captain.

BURIDAN

Take it—in this pocket.

LANDRY

Then?

BURIDAN

How many pounds do you make a year?

LANDRY

Six pounds.

BURIDAN

Count what's in the purse while I consider.

(pause)

Have you counted?

LANDRY

Have you considered?

BURIDAN

Yes—how much is there?

LANDRY

Three gold marks.

BURIDAN

One hundred sixty-five gold pounds—listen, you would have to spend twenty-eight years of your life in this prison to earn that sum. Swear to me on your eternal salvation, to do what I am going to tell you—and this sum is yours. It's all I possess. If I had more, I would give you more.

LANDRY

And you?

BURIDAN

If they hang me, which is likely, the executioner will bear the cost of my interment and I have no need of this sum. If I escape which is possible, you will have four times this sum—and I a thousand.

LANDRY

What must be done, Captain?

BURIDAN

A very simple thing. You can leave the Chalet. And when you leave, never return again.

LANDRY

I ask nothing better.

BURIDAN

You will lodge with Pierre de Bourges, the Tavenkeeper at Les Innocents—that's where I am lodging. You will ask for the Captain's room. They will give you mine.

LANDRY

Up to this point, it doesn't seem difficult.

BURIDAN

Listen—once in my room, you will shut yourself in. You will count the flagstones which pave it to the corner where there is a crucifix.

(Landry nods)

Listen to me then. On the seventh you will see a cross. You will pull it up with your knife and under a black bed you will find a letter box the key to which is in this purse. You can open it to see that it contains papers and not money. Then, tomorrow at the moment the King returns to Paris, if you haven't seen me, safe and sound and if I haven't said, "Return that box and that key" you will hand them both to Louis X, King of France—and if I am dead, you will have avenged me. That's all—my soul will be at peace, and it is up to you that I will owe it.

LANDRY

And I run no other risk?

BURIDAN

None at all.

LANDRY

You can count on me.

BURIDAN

On your eternal salvation promise to do what I have told you?

LANDRY

I swear it on the role I hope for in Paradise.

BURIDAN

Then, goodbye Landry. Be an honest man if you can.

LANDRY

I will do what I can, my Captain, but it is very difficult.

(He leaves.)

BURIDAN

Come, come. Let the executioner and the rope come—vengeance is seated at the foot of the gallows. Vengeance, a joyous and sublime word when it is pronounced by a living mouth, a sonorous and empty word pronounced over a tomb, and which as loud as it resounds doesn't wake the cadaver sleeping in the grave.

(Marguerite, with Orsini enters by a secret door, holding a lamp in her hand.)

MARGUERITE

Is he chained so I can approach him without fear?

ORSINI

Yes, Madame.

MARGUERITE

Well—wait for me there, Orsini, and at the least cry, come to me.

(Orsini leaves.)

BURIDAN

A light. Someone's coming.

MARGUERITE

(approaching)

Yes, someone! Didn't you expect to see someone before death?

BURIDAN

(laughing)

I hoped for it; but I didn't count on it. Ah, Marguerite, you said to yourself, "He cannot die without my rejoicing in triumph, without knowing that it's really me who is killing him." Woman of all sensuality—to me, to me. Yes, Marguerite, yes, I had counted on your presence—you were right.

MARGUERITE

But without hope, right? You know me enough to know that after having reduced me to fear, abused me to beg, that neither fears nor prayers will move my heart. Oh, your measures were well taken Buridan—only you forgot that love, lawless love, enters in a man's heart and it overcomes all other sentiments, it lives despite honor, faith, oaths and you confided in an oath, in faith, in the honor of an amorous man—amorous of me—the proof, the only proof you had against me. Here—here's your precious page from your notebook, "I die murdered by the hand of Marguerite—Philippe D'Aulnay." The last goodbye between brothers, and the brother gave it to me. Here, here, look.

(taking the lamp)

Die, with this last flame, your last hope! Am I free now, Buridan? Can I do with you what I wish?

BURIDAN

What are you going to do?

MARGUERITE

Aren't you arrested as the murderer of Philippe D'Aulnay? What does one do with murderers?

BURIDAN

And what court has judged me without hearing me?

MARGUERITE

A court? But you are mad! How do they judge men who bear such secrets? There are poisons so violent that they break the bottle that contains them. Your secret is one of those poisons, Buridan. When a man like you is arrested, he is chained, as you are chained—and they put him in a deep cell like this. If they don't want to lose time, from the moment he enters his prison, a priest and an executioner are brought. The priest begins. In this prison, there is an iron axe, like this—some walls, too, which extinguish tears, and absorb agony. The priest leaves first. Then the executioner follows and then when, the next day, the jailor comes in he goes back frightened—saying that the condemned man whose hands were imprudently left free has strangled himself—which is proof of his guilt.

BURIDAN

I see that we are at least frank, Marguerite, I have told you my plans and you have told me yours.

MARGUERITE

You jest, or rather intend to jest; your pride revolts at my victory; you want to let me believe that you have some way to escape me, to torment my sleep or my pleasures; but no, no, your smile doesn't disturb me, the damn laugh also—to pretend there is no remorse. No, you cannot escape me, right? It is impossible—you are chained—these walls are very thick, these doors very solid, no, no, you cannot escape me and I am going. Adieu, Buridan, have you something to tell me?

BURIDAN

One thing only.

MARGUERITE

Speak.

BURIDAN

It's a memory of youth that I want to tell you about. In 1293, twenty years ago. Bourgogne was happy—for she had the beloved Duke Robert II for Duke—don't interrupt me. The Duke Robert had a young and beautiful daughter, with the looks of an angel and the soul of a demon. They called her Marguerite de Bourgogne—let me finish—the Duke Robert had a young and handsome page, open hearted and trusting with blond hair and rosy complexion. He was named Lyonnet de Bourneville. Ah, you listen with attention it seems to me. The page and the young girl loved each other. Whoever saw them, at that time and saw them now wouldn't recognize them and perhaps, if they met, they wouldn't recognize each other.

MARGUERITE

Where is all this leading?

BURIDAN

Oh—you are going to see. It's a bizarre story. The page and the young girl loved each other, unknown to all the world. Each night a ladder of silk led the lover to the arms if his mistress, and each night the lover and the mistress made a rendezvous for the following night. Then one day, the daughter of Duke Robert announced, crying to Lyonnet de Bourneville, that she was going to be a mother.

MARGUERITE

Great God!

BURIDAN

Help me to change my position, Marguerite. This position tires me.

(she helps him, he laughs)

Thanks—where was I, Marguerite?

MARGUERITE

The daughter of the Duke was going to be a mother.

BURIDAN

Ah, yes—that's it. Eight days later, the secret was no more, for her father, the Duke announced to his daughter that the next day the doors of a convent would open for her and would close on her forever. That night, the lovers reunited. Oh—it was a frightful night. Lyonnet loved Marguerite, the gay Gaultier loved her, a night of tears and curses. Oh—young Marguerite, what she promised to be, and what she has been.

MARGUERITE

And afterwards! Afterwards!

BURIDAN

These cords hurt my flesh and make me ill, Marguerite.

(Marguerite cuts the cords, he looks at her and laughs)

She held a dagger, just as you do, the young Marguerite, and she said, "Lyonnet, Lyonnet, yes, between now and tomorrow, my father must die, there will be no more convent, no more separation; there will only be love." I don't know what was done but the dagger passed into the hands of Lyonnet de Bourneville, an arm led him, escorted him in the shadows, raised a curtain, and the page, armed and the Duke, asleep, found themselves face-to-face.

The old boy had a noble head, calm and beautiful, as the assassin had seen many times in his dreams, for the infamous one assassinated him, but Marguerite, the young and beautiful Marguerite didn't enter the convent, and she became Queen of Navarre, then of France. The next day, the page received from a man named Orsini, a letter and some gold. Marguerite begged him to go away forever. She said that after their common crime, they could never see each other anymore!

MARGUERITE

Imprudent!

BURIDAN

Yes, imprudent, right? For this letter, entirely in her writing, signed by her, reproduced the crime in all its details and all her complicity. Queen Marguerite would never make a mistake like young imprudent Marguerite, would she?

MARGUERITE

Well, Lyonnet de Bourneville left, right? And no one knows what has become of him—he will never be seen again. The letter is lost or destroyed, and cannot be a proof. What can Marguerite, the Queen Regent of France have to do with the story?

BURIDAN

Lyonnet de Bourneville isn't dead; and you know it very well, Marguerite, for I saw you tremble when you recognized him.

MARGUERITE

And the letter? The letter?

BURIDAN

The letter will be offered to the King of France, Louis X, on his return.

MARGUERITE

You say this to frighten me, right? It cannot be; you would have used this way first.

BURIDAN

You took care to furnish me another—I reserved this for a

second occasion.

MARGUERITE

The letter?

BURIDAN

Tomorrow your husband will get it. You have told me the fate of a murderer, Marguerite. Do you know the fate of a parricide and adulteress? Listen, first they shave their hair with red hot scissors, then they tear open their breast to tear out their hearts. They burn it, then they throw the ashes to the wind and for three days they drag the body around the city on a sled.

MARGUERITE

Mercy! Mercy!

BURIDAN

Come, come, a last service, Marguerite, untie the cords.

(he holds his hands and she unties them)

Ah—it is good to be free. Let the executioner come now. Here are the ropes. Well—what's wrong, tomorrow, in the city then will say—"Buridan, the murderer of Philippe D'Aulnay strangled himself in his prison." Another will reply. "Marguerite de Bourgogne has been condemned to the penalty for adulteresses and parricides."

MARGUERITE

Grace, Buridan.

BURIDAN

I am no longer Buridan. I am Lyonnet de Bourneville, the page of Marguerite—the assassin of Duke Robert.

MARGUERITE

Don't talk so loud!

BURIDAN

And what can you fear? These walls stifle cries, extinguish tears, absorb agony.

MARGUERITE

What do you want? What do you want?

BURIDAN

When you return tomorrow on the right side of the King as he enters Paris, I wish to be at his left—we shall go before him together.

MARGUERITE

We will go together.

BURIDAN

That's fine.

MARGUERITE

And this letter?

BURIDAN

Well—when it is presented, I will take it after all, I shall be Prime Minister.

MARGUERITE

Marigny is not yet dead.

BURIDAN

Yesterday, at Orsini's tavern, you swore to me that by the tenth hour it would be done.

MARGUERITE

I still have an hour, it's more than enough to accomplish my promise—and I am going to give the order.

BURIDAN

Wait, one last question, Marguerite, the children of Marguerite and Lyonnet—what became of them?

MARGUERITE

I entrusted them to a man.

BURIDAN

The name of this man?

MARGUERITE

I don't remember it.

BURIDAN

Search, Marguerite, and you will recall it.

MARGUERITE

Orsini, I believe.

BURIDAN

(calling)

Orsini! Orsini!

MARGUERITE

What are you doing?

BURIDAN

Isn't he here?

MARGUERITE

No.

(Orsini enters.)

BURIDAN

Here he is! Come here, Orsini. Tomorrow, I am Prime Minister. You don't believe it? Tell him, Madame, so he will believe it.

MARGUERITE

It's the truth.

BURIDAN

The first act of mine will be to put to the question a certain Orsini who was at the Court of Duke Robert.

ORSINI

And why, Milord, why?

BURIDAN

To know from him how he carried out the orders given to him by Marguerite de Bourgogne relative to the two children.

ORSINI

Oh! Pardon, Milord, pardon, for not having put them to death, as I was ordered.

MARGUERITE

It was not I who gave that order—it was—

BURIDAN

Shut up, Marguerite.

ORSINI

Pardon if I lacked the courage—they were two boys so weak and handsome.

BURIDAN

What did you do with them, wretch?

ORSINI

I gave them to one of my men to expose them—and I said they were dead.

BURIDAN

And this man?

ORSINI

One of the jailers of this prison—he's called Landry—pardon.

BURIDAN

That's fine, Orsini—there's a trait which does you honor. An idea came to you which didn't come to a mother—you didn't have to kill the children, when you could expose them. Orsini, had you committed many crimes, there is an action which redeems you—you still have a heart. Embrace me, Orsini—oh, you will have gold which weighs as much as those children—two boys, right? Oh, my children, my children! Ah—enough, enough, you see how the Queen takes pity on me.

ORSINI

What remains for me to do, Milord?

BURIDAN

Take this lamp, and light up the way—take my arm, Madame.

MARGUERITE

Where are we going?

BURIDAN

To meet King Louis X, who will return to his good city of Paris tomorrow.

CURTAIN

ACT IV: BURIDAN
SCENE 7

A hall in the Louvre—door in the back, two side doors—further front two more side doors.

GAULTIER

(enters)

Marguerite! Marguerite! She cannot yet have left her chamber.

CHARLOTTE

(appearing in the Queen's door)

Is it you, Madame? The Lord Gaultier!

GAULTIER

Charlotte, I hope our sovereign, may God preserve her—is in good health?

CHARLOTTE

I don't know, Milord; I left her chamber.

GAULTIER

Well.

CHARLOTTE

It hasn't been slept in.

GAULTIER

What are you saying, Charlotte?

CHARLOTTE

The truth! Ah, my God, I am very worried.

GAULTIER

What do you say?

CHARLOTTE

I say, Milord, that when I came to see her, the Queen wasn't in this room.

GAULTIER

The Queen is not yet in her apartment, she isn't here; she isn't in the palace—oh, my God—but don't you know anything child, don't you know anything that could tell us where she might be?

CHARLOTTE

Yesterday evening, she asked me for her cloak to go out, and I haven't seen her since.

GAULTIER

You haven't seen her? But perhaps you know where she went? Tell me, I'll run after her, so that I may know what has happened to her, so I can find her.

CHARLOTTE

I don't know where she went, Milord.

GAULTIER

Listen, fear nothing—if it's a secret she had confided to you, tell me, for she confides in me all her secrets; don't be afraid, repeat it to me, all you know. I will tell her that I forced you to tell me and she will pardon you; and I, I, Charlotte, you will extract a dagger from my heart; right—she told you where she went.

CHARLOTTE

She told me nothing about it, I swear it to you.

GAULTIER

Yes, yes, she told you to be discreet; you do well, child, to protect her—but I, I know you know she would have told me, just as she told you where she went—tell me—tell me. Wait, do you want something you cannot hope to have in this world?

CHARLOTTE

I want nothing except to know what has become of the Queen.

GAULTIER

Ask what you wish, and tell me where she is for you must know, right? Ask what you wish—some jewels, I will get them for you; do you have a poor fiancé?—I will give him dowry money. Do you want him to be near you? I will pass him through my guards. What the daughter of a count or a baron could not hope for, you shall have—for a single reply—Charlotte, where is the Queen, where is Marguerite?

CHARLOTTE

Alas! Alas! Milord, I don't know—but perhaps.

GAULTIER

Speak! Speak!

CHARLOTTE

This Italian, Orsini—

GAULTIER

Yes, yes, you are right, Charlotte and I shall run—oh, if she returns in my absence, tell her to give me a moment before the reentry of the King—you will beg her, right? You will tell her that it is I, I am her faithful and devoted servant who begs it; you will tell her I am in despair—that I will go mad if she doesn't say a word to me, a word which will reassure and console me.

CHARLOTTE

Leave, leave—they're coming to open the apartments.

GAULTIER

Yes. Yes.

CHARLOTTE

Courage, Milord! I am going to pray for you.

(Gaultier leaves and Charlotte returns to the Queen's apartment.)

(Enter Savoisy, Pierrefonds, Lords.)

SAVOISY

Aren't you going to appear before the King, Lord de Pierrefonds?

PIERREFONDS

No, Milord, if the Queen is going, I will accompany her—and you?

SAVOISY

I will await our Lord here; on the way there's such an abundance of people that one cannot pass—I don't wish to be confounded with the roughnecks.

PIERREFONDS

And then you thought that the true King is not Louis Le Huton, but Marguerite de Bourgogne, so better pay court to Marguerite than to Louis.

SAVOISY

Perhaps, something like that.

(to Raoul, who enters)

Hello, Baron, what news?

RAOUL

The King is coming here, Milords.

SAVOISY

And the Queen hasn't appeared.

RAOUL

The Queen has gone to him and is entering on his right.

PHILIPPE

(outside)

Long live the King! Long live the King!

RAOUL

Wait—do you hear the cries of the roughnecks?

SAVOISY

We have made a mistake.

RAOUL

But perhaps I will really astonish you if I tell you who is on his left?

SAVOISY

By God! It would be a surprise if it was anyone other than

Gaultier D'Aulnay!

RAOUL

Gaultier D'Aulnay isn't even in the procession.

SAVOISY

He isn't in the procession, he isn't here—was he at the feast last night at the Tower of Nesle, is it that he would make another body or two on the waves of the Seine? Well—who was at the left of the King?

RAOUL

Milords, at his left, on a superb horse, this Italian Captain, who we saw arrested yesterday by Gaultier, under the balcony of Louis and escorted to the Chalet.

SAVOISY

It's impossible.

RAOUL

You are going to see.

PIERREFONDS

What do you say to this, Savoisy?

SAVOISY

I say that we live in very strange times. Yesterday Marigny was Prime Minister, today Marigny is arrested. Yesterday, the Captain was arrested, perhaps today this Captain will be Prime

Minister. On my honor, one could believe that God was playing with Satan for this beautiful realm of France.

PEOPLE

(outside)

Long live the King!

PIERREFONDS

And here the people who are so restless; who care so little; who is arrested; or who is Prime Minister who cry long live the King.

(Lords entering.)

LORDS

The King, gentlemen, the King.

PEOPLE

Long live the King.

KING

(entering)

Greetings, Milords, greetings, we are happy to have left in Champagne such a fine army and to find waiting here such a fine nobility.

SAVOISY

Lord, they say it will be a great day for us when you join the Army with the nobility to march against the enemy.

KING

And to help you make the expenses of the campaign, gentlemen, I am going to order a special tax be levied on the city of Paris on the occasion of my return.

PEOPLE

Long live the King! Long live the King!

KING

(going to the balcony)

Yes, my children—I am busy lessening the customs duties—I want you to be happy—for I love you.

BURIDAN

(to the Queen)

Recall our agreement—to us the power, the two of us rule France.

MARGUERITE

Count on taking your place today with me in council.

BURIDAN

Be of my opinion, I will be of yours.

PEOPLE

Long live the King! Long live the King!

KING

(from the balcony)

Yes, yes, my children.

(turning toward Buridan)

You hear Lord Lyonnet de Bourneville? You will prepare a new relief on the estates and workers of the city of Paris so that each may pay for this new tax what he paid for the other; that will be just.

SAVOISY

Lyonnet de Bourneville! It appears this is not a soldier of fortune. That's an old name.

KING

We will enter into council. Milords, before taking leave of you, here is my hand to kiss.

(He sits on an armchair brought up by a page and is surrounded by courtiers on both sides.)

GAULTIER

(enters quickly)

The Queen! They told me—here she is!

MARGUERITE

Gaultier—approach Lord Captain and kiss the hand of the King.

(low as he passes in front of her)

I love you. I only love you, I will love you forever.

GAULTIER

Buridan! Buridan here!

MARGUERITE

Silence.

(Landry appears on the balcony.)

BURIDAN

Landry!

LANDRY

(pointing to the iron box)

Captain.

BURIDAN

You see!

LANDRY

Indeed!

BURIDAN

The box?

LANDRY

The dozen gold marks?

BURIDAN

This evening I will bring them to you.

LANDRY

Where?

BURIDAN

At my old lodging, in the tavern of Pierre de Bourges.

LANDRY

This evening, I will return you the box.

BURIDAN

I have to ask you many things.

LANDRY

I will answer to you for everything.

BURIDAN

That's fine.

(to guards)

Make these people move off.

GUARDS

Back, roughnecks, back.

SOME PEOPLE

Long live the King! Long live the King!

(The people cling to the balcony. The guards push them down with blows of the halberd handles.)

KING

Now, let's concern ourselves with affairs of the realm. Good day, gentlemen.

AN OFFICER

Place for the King! Place for the Queen! Place for the Prime Minister.

(King, Queen and Buridan pass out with Royal Counselors. The guards leave.)

SAVOISY

Are we awake or are we sleeping, gentlemen? As for me, I am going to install myself here.

(sits down)

If I am sleeping, I will awaken. If I am awake, they'll kick me out. But I intend to know the end of the thing.

PIERREFONDS

If we were to ask Gaultier—perhaps he is in on the secret, Gaultier?

GAULTIER

(throwing himself in an armchair on the other side)

Oh, leave me alone, gentlemen. I know nothing, I can figure out nothing. Leave me alone, I beg you.

SAVOISY

The door is opening.

OFFICER

(coming forward)

The Lord de Pierrefonds.

PIERREFONDS

Here.

OFFICER

Order of the King.

(The officer leaves. All the courtiers group around Pierrefonds.)

PIERREFONDS

(reading)

"Order to take the Sire Enguerrand de Marigny from Vincennes to escort him to Montfaucon."

SAVOISY

Fine! The King has put his signature to an arrest and execution—that's promising. Many compliments on your mission.

PIERREFONDS

I would much prefer another, but what is must be. I will go do it. Goodbye, gentlemen.

(He leaves.)

SAVOISY

Well—we are sure of one thing—that the Prime Minister will always be hanged. The King had promised to do something for his people.

(The officer returns.)

OFFICER

The Lord the Count de Savoisy.

SAVOISY

Here.

OFFICER

Letters patent from the King.

(He leaves. All the courtiers approach Savoisy.)

ALL

Let's see. Let's see.

SAVOISY

God's blood, gentlemen—you are in a greater hurry than I am. The first order makes me in no hurry to open the second and if by chance it was one of you I must take to hang that would make me somewhat unwilling to hurry—

(slowly opens his parchment)

My commission as Captain in the Guards, you know of a vacancy, gentlemen?

RAOUL

No—unless Gaultier.

SAVOISY

(looking at Gaultier)

By God—you are making me think—

RAOUL

Never mind! Accept our congratulations.

SAVOISY

Fine, gentlemen, fine. I must instantly take my post in the apartments. Stay here, if it's your good pleasure, gentlemen. Gentlemen, on my part, I have learned what I wanted to know.

(laughing)

The King is a great King and the new minister is a great man.

(He leaves. The officer enters.)

OFFICER

Sire Gaultier D'Aulnay!

GAULTIER

Huh?

OFFICER

Letters patent from the King.

GAULTIER

(rising)

From the King!

(He takes them, astonished.)

OFFICER

Milords, the King our lord won't receive after the council meeting. You may retire.

GAULTIER

(reading)

"Letters patent from the King, giving to the Lord D'Aulnay

the command of the county of Champagne," me to command a Province! "Order to leave Paris and report to Troyes." Me, leave Paris?

RAOUL

Sire D'Aulnay, we congratulate you. Justice is done and the Queen could not make a better choice.

GAULTIER

Congratulate Satan! For the Archangel became the King of Hell.

(tearing the orders)

I will not leave.

(to the Lords)

Didn't the King tell you you could retire, gentlemen?

RAOUL

And you?

GAULTIER

I—? I am staying!

RAOUL

If we don't see you before your departure, bon voyage, Lord Gaultier.

GAULTIER

God protect you!

(The Courtiers leave.)

GAULTIER

(alone)

To leave—to leave, to quit Paris. Is that what they promised me? But who can tell me on what land I have been walking for several days? Around me is nothing but deception, every object appears real to me but when I touch it, it disappears between my hands—Phantoms!

MARGUERITE

(coming in from the rear)

Good afternoon!

GAULTIER

Ah, then it is you, Madame.

MARGUERITE

Silence!

GAULTIER

For long enough I have been silent, I must speak to you even if each word cost me a year of my life. Do you mock me, Marguerite, to promise and, at the same time, retract your word? Am I a toy to be played with? Am I a child to be laughed at? Yesterday, you swore to me that nothing would separate us and today they are sending me far from Paris to I don't know what country.

MARGUERITE

Have you received the King's order?

GAULTIER

(pointing to the scraps on the ground)

And there it is, behold!

MARGUERITE

Calm down.

GAULTIER

You were able to approve this order?

MARGUERITE

I was forced to.

GAULTIER

Forced to! And by whom? Who can force the Queen?

MARGUERITE

A demon who has me in his power.

GAULTIER

But what is he? Tell me?

MARGUERITE

Pretend to obey and perhaps between now and tomorrow I can see you and explain everything.

GAULTIER

And you want me to withdraw on such an assurance?

MARGUERITE

You won't have to leave; but go away, go away!

GAULTIER

I will return. I must have an explanation of this secret.

MARGUERITE

Yes, yes, you will return; here's someone, someone's coming.

GAULTIER

Remember your promise. Goodbye.

(He hurries out.)

MARGUERITE

Just in time!

BURIDAN

(entering)

Pardon me if I interrupted your goodbyes, Marguerite.

MARGUERITE

You've seen ill, Buridan.

BURIDAN

Wasn't that Gaultier leaving?

MARGUERITE

Since you've seen ill, it wasn't goodbye.

BURIDAN

How's that?

MARGUERITE

It's that he won't leave.

BURIDAN

The King has ordered him.

MARGUERITE

And I, I forbid him.

BURIDAN

Marguerite, are you forgetting our agreement?

MARGUERITE

I promised you to make you Prime Minister and I kept my word—you promised to leave me Gaultier and you exact his departure.

BURIDAN

We said, "We two will rule France," and not "we three"—this young man would make a third in our power and secrets, it's impossible.

MARGUERITE

He still will be.

BURIDAN

Have you forgotten you were in my power?

MARGUERITE

Yes, yesterday, you were only Buridan the prisoner, today you are only Lyonnet de Bourneville, Prime Minister.

BURIDAN

What's the point?

MARGUERITE

You cannot destroy me without destroying yourself.

BURIDAN

Would that have stopped me yesterday?

MARGUERITE

It will stop you today. Yesterday you had everything to gain and nothing to lose except your life. Today, with your life, you will lose honors, rank, fortune, power. You will fall from a high position, right? In the hope of bringing me down, in your fall you will decide to hurl yourself down! We have arrived together at the height of a mountain peak, sharp and icy. Believe me, Buridan, let's help each other rather than threaten both of us.

BURIDAN

You really love him then?

MARGUERITE

More than my life.

BURIDAN

Love in the heart of Marguerite! I would have thought one could press it and twist it and not find a single human feeling. You are less than what I hoped you to be. If we wish, Marguerite, then nothing can stop our will which tells us where to go. It's necessary that this will be very strong to break anything it encounters in its way, without costing a tear in our eye or a regret in our heart. We have become things which govern, and not creatures which soften—oh, misfortune, misfortune to you, Marguerite! I believed you a demon and you are only a fallen angel!

MARGUERITE

Listen, if it is not from love, invent a name for my weakness—but don't let him go, I beg you.

BURIDAN

(aside)

There would be two against me, that's too many.

MARGUERITE

What are you saying?

BURIDAN

(aside)

I destroy myself if I destroy them.

(aloud)

Let him stay?

MARGUERITE

Yes—I beg you.

BURIDAN

And if I were jealous of him?

MARGUERITE

You—jealous?

BURIDAN

If the memory of what I was to you makes the thought intolerable that another is loved more by you; if what you took for ambition, for hate, for vengeance, if all that was love which I couldn't extinguish and which reproduces itself in all its forms. If I don't want to show what will happen to you, if now that I have arrived. I want nothing but you, if my ancient rights, rights preceding his, I would sacrifice everything for you, if in exchange for one of those nights where the page Lyonnet slid trembling into the bed of the young Marguerite, not to leave until the break of day, I would give you the letters to which I owe the position I have arrived at, if I would deliver to you my means of establishing my fortune to prove that my fortune has only one end, and that attained, the rest matters little, speak, speak if you would find in me this devotion, this love—wouldn't you agree to let him leave?

MARGUERITE

Are you speaking sincerely or are you jesting, Lyonnet?

BURIDAN

A rendezvous, this evening and this evening I will surrender your letters to you; but no more, Marguerite, a rendezvous like that in the tavern or the prison. No more a rendezvous of hate, but a rendezvous of love. And tomorrow, tomorrow you can keep him and betray me, since once that is done my strength will be at an end.

MARGUERITE

But, even supposing that I consent to it, I cannot receive you in this place.

BURIDAN

Can't you leave when you wish to see him?

MARGUERITE

Can I without ruining myself, see you as well?

BURIDAN

The Tower of Nesle.

MARGUERITE

You would come there?

BURIDAN

Didn't I go there already without knowing what to expect?

MARGUERITE

(aside)

He's delivering himself into my hands—

(aloud)

Listen, Buridan, it's a strange weakness; but if you see me recall all the moments of joy your voice awakes, so many memories of love that I believed dead in the depths of my heart.

BURIDAN

Marguerite!

MARGUERITE

Lyonnet.

BURIDAN

Gaultier will leave tomorrow?

MARGUERITE

I will tell you tonight.

(giving him the key)

Here is the key to the Tower—let us separate.

(aside)

Ah, Buridan, if you escape me this time—

(She leaves.)

BURIDAN

This is the key to your fall, Marguerite, but rest easy, I won't shut you in there all alone.

(He leaves. Marguerite returns and goes to a side door.)

MARGUERITE

Orsini! Orsini!

ORSINI

Here I am, Queen.

MARGUERITE

This evening, at the Tower of Nesle, four armed men and you.

ORSINI

Have you any other orders?

MARGUERITE

Not for the moment. I will tell you there what you have to do. Go.

(Orsini leaves.)

MARGUERITE

No one—that's fine.

(She leaves. Buridan enters from another side door, a parchment in his hand.)

BURIDAN

Count de Savoisy! Count de Savoisy!

SAVOISY

Here I am, Milord.

BURIDAN

The King has learned with pain of the massacres which desolate his good city of Paris—he thinks and rightly so, that the murderers meet at the Tower of Nesle. This evening at 9:30, you will surround it with ten men and you will arrest all those that you find there—whoever they may be, regardless of their title or their rank. Here is the order.

SAVOISY

Well, I won't be late to carry out this duty.

BURIDAN

And you may say it is the most important you will ever fulfill!

(He leaves by a side door and Savoisy by the other.)

CURTAIN

ACT V:
GAULTIER D'AULNAY
SCENE 8

The Tavern of Pierre de Bourges

Landry enters counting.

LANDRY

Twelve gold marks. This done, if I count right, six hundred and eight pounds. If the Captain keeps his word and gives me this sum in exchange for this little iron box for which I wouldn't give six sous, I can follow his advice and become an honest man. Now we must do something. What should I do? My word, with my money I shall raise a company. I will be commander. I will put myself in the service of some great lord; I will pocket all my money and I will make my men live off the land. Praise God! It will be a situation lacking in neither wine nor women. Then, if some pilgrim or merchant passes who is full of too much gold or merchandise, as the kingdom of heaven is always for the poor—why, we will help him enter. God's blood, there, if I don't deceive myself, is a happy and honest life and one which permits one to faithfully accomplish his duties as a Christian, and burn, from time to time some gypsy and burn some Jew—the blessing appears to me so easy as to drink a glass of wine. Ah—here is the Captain.

(Buridan enters.)

BURIDAN

It's real, Landry.

LANDRY

You see, I am waiting for you.

BURIDAN

And you're drinking while waiting for me?

LANDRY

I don't know a better companion than wine.

BURIDAN

(pulling out his purse)

Yes—it's the gold with which one buys it.

LANDRY

Here's the box.

BURIDAN

Here are your twelve gold marks.

LANDRY

Thanks.

BURIDAN

Now, I have given a rendezvous here to a young man. He's going to come. Leave me this room for a while. As soon as you see him, leave. Return as I want to talk with you.

(A noise on the stairway.)

LANDRY

By God, he follows you closely. Wait, he's breaking his neck on the stairs.

BURIDAN

Good! Leave us.

GAULTIER

(at the door)

Captain Buridan.

LANDRY

Here he is.

(Landry opens and leaves. Gaultier enters.)

BURIDAN

(smiling)

I thought you knew my new title and my new name; Sir Gaultier? I am deceived, it seems—since this morning they call me Lyonnet de Bourneville and Prime Minister.

GAULTIER

Little matter, what name you are called or what your title is—you are a man that summons other men on their word—are you prepared to fulfill it?

BURIDAN

I promised to let you know the murderer of your brother.

GAULTIER

Not just that; you promised me something else.

BURIDAN

I promised to tell you how Enguerrand de Marigny went in one day from the Louvre to the gallows at Montfaucon.

GAULTIER

That's not it. Be he guilty or not, it is between his judges and God. You promised me something else.

BURIDAN

Was it to teach you how a man arrested by you yesterday become Prime Minister today?

GAULTIER

No, no. Whether this method comes from God or Satan is of little consequence—there's in all this some terrible secrets which I don't want to know. My brother is dead; God will avenge him. Marigny is dead; God will judge him. It's not that. You promised me something else.

BURIDAN

Explain yourself.

GAULTIER

You promised to make me see Marguerite.

BURIDAN

How your love for this woman chokes all other sentiments. Fraternal amity is no more than a word. Bloody intrigues of the court are nothing but a game. Oh, you are really senseless.

GAULTIER

You promised to make me see Marguerite.

BURIDAN

Do you need me for that? Can't you enter the secret door in the alcove, or do you tremble that tonight, like the last night? Marguerite will not return to the Louvre.

GAULTIER

(overwhelmed)

Who told you that?

BURIDAN

I was the one with whom Marguerite spent the night.

GAULTIER

Blasphemer! But it is you who are mad, Buridan.

BURIDAN

Calm yourself child, don't worry your sword in its scabbard. Marguerite is beautiful and passionate, right? What did she tell you when you asked her how she got that scratch in her cheek.

GAULTIER

My God! My God! Take pity on me.

BURIDAN

Without doubt, she wrote to you.

GAULTIER

What does it matter to you?

BURIDAN

She has an ardent and magical bewitching style with which she draws her passion, right?

GAULTIER

Your damned eyes have never seen the sacred writing of the queen, I hope?

BURIDAN

(opening the iron box)

You recognize it? Read "your beloved Marguerite."

GAULTIER

It's magic—it's hellish.

BURIDAN

Not when she's nearby, when she speaks of love, not when it's sweet to put your hand in her long hair which she lets float voluptuously—and you cut a tress like this one here?

(He pulls a lock of hair from the box.)

GAULTIER

It's her writing—the color of her hair. Tell me how you have stolen this letter—tell me how you cut her hair by trick?

BURIDAN

You will ask her herself; I promised to make you see her.

GAULTIER

Right now! Right now!

BURIDAN

But perhaps she isn't yet at the rendezvous.

GAULTIER

A rendezvous! Who has a rendezvous with her? Name him—oh, I thirst for his life's blood.

BURIDAN

Ingrate—and if that person were to cede his place to you?

GAULTIER

To me?

BURIDAN

Yes—perhaps from lassitude, perhaps from compassion for you. He no longer wants this woman—if he cedes her, if he surrenders her, if he gives her to you.

GAULTIER

(drawing his dagger)

Ah—curse!

BURIDAN

Young man.

GAULTIER

Oh, my God—pity.

BURIDAN

It is 8:30. Marguerite is waiting. Gaultier, will you make her wait?

GAULTIER

Where is she?

BURIDAN

At the Tower of Nesle.

GAULTIER

Very good.

(He starts to leave.)

BURIDAN

You are forgetting the key.

GAULTIER

Give it here.

BURIDAN

One word more.

GAULTIER

Speak.

BURIDAN

She killed your brother.

GAULTIER

Damnation.

(He disappears.)

BURIDAN

Fine, go rejoin her, and destroy each other. That's fine. Yes, if Savoisy is as punctual as they are, they will be strange prisoners. Now, I need to know only one thing—what has become of those two wretched children? Oh, if I had them to split my fortune with, and to rely on them. Landry will have to be very clever if I don't learn from him what became of them. Here he is now.

(Landry enters.)

LANDRY

You have something to say to me, Captain?

BURIDAN

Oh, nothing—tell me, how much time will it take that young man to go from here to the Tower of Nesle.

LANDRY

There are no boats now; he'll have to go to the Mill Bridge—it's a half hour to there or a little less.

BURIDAN

That's good. Put this on the table. I want to discuss an old acquaintance. Landry, our war is in Italy. Take a glass and sit down.

LANDRY

Yes, yes, they were rough wars, yet a good time. The days were spent in battles; the nights in orgies. You recall, Captain, the wines of the rich Prior of Genes which we drank to the last drop; the convent of young girls which we despoiled to last nun, all these things are happy memories, but great sins, Captain.

BURIDAN

At the day of death, they will put our sins on the side of good actions and balance them against each other. I hope you have made enough provisions for these.

LANDRY

Yes, yes, I have several meritorious works in which I hope.

(They drink.)

BURIDAN

Tell me, then, they will edify me.

LANDRY

In the trial of the Templars, there was needed a witness to make God's cause triumph and to condemn Jacques de Molay, the Grand Master. A worthy Benedictine cast his eyes on me and dictated a false testimony that I repeated under oath word for word before the judges as if it were true. On the next day, the heretics were burned to the great Glory of God and our Holy Religion.

BURIDAN

Continue my brave—someone told me a story about some children.

(They drink.)

LANDRY

Yes, that was in Germany. Poor little angel. I hope that he'll pray in heaven for me. Imagine, Captain, we were hunting gypsies, who are, you know, pagan, idolaters, and infidels, we traversed their village, which was all afire. I heard crying from a burning house. I went in. There was a poor little abandoned gypsy baby. I looked around. I found water in a vase and I baptized him as a Christian, which was good. I went to put him in a place where the fire wouldn't reach him, but I reflected the next day the relative would return, and the devil with the baptism. I put him back in his cradle and I rejoined my comrades. Behind me, the roof collapsed.

BURIDAN

(distracted)

And the child perished?

LANDRY

Yes, but who was fooled? It's Satan who comes to take an idolater's soul and who burns his fingers touch a Christian.

BURIDAN

Yes, I see that you have always had properly instructed religion, but I want to speak to you of other children—of the two children that Orsini—

LANDRY

I know what you want to say.

BURIDAN

Yes.

LANDRY

Yes, yes, they were two poor little ones that Orsini told me to throw in the water like cats, who can't yet see, and that I was tempted to keep alive, although he assured me they were Christians.

BURIDAN

(quickly)

And what did you do with them?

LANDRY

I exposed them in the outer sanctuary of Notre Dame where one customarily puts these little creatures.

BURIDAN

Do you know what became of them?

LANDRY

No. I know they were accepted, that's all; for by evening, they were gone.

BURIDAN

And didn't you put some sign on them so they could be recognized?

LANDRY

Indeed, indeed, I fixed them. They were crying very hard, but it was for their good—I did it with a dagger—a cross on their left arms.

BURIDAN

A red cross? A cross on the left arm? Same cross on the both of them? Oh, say it wasn't a cross that you made; say it wasn't on the left arm. Say you put some other sign on them.

LANDRY

It was a cross and nothing else; it was on the left arm and no other place.

BURIDAN

Oh, misfortune, misfortune, my children, Philippe, Gaultier! The one dead, the other near death. Both murdered—one by her, the other by me! Justice of God, Landry where can we get a barge, so we can get there before this young man?

LANDRY

At Simon the Fisherman's.

BURIDAN

Then, a ladder, a sword and follow me.

LANDRY

Where to, Captain?

BURIDAN

To the Tower of Nesle. Misfortune!

CURTAIN

ACT V
SCENE 9

The Tower of Nesle.

MARGUERITE

You understand, Orsini? It is a last necessity—it's still another murder, but the last. This man knows all our secrets of life or death, yours and mine. If I hadn't struggled for the last three days against him to the point of exhaustion with him, we would already both have been lost.

ORSINI

But this man then has demons at his orders, to be instructed there in all we have done.

MARGUERITE

Small matter how he learned it, but now he knows. With a word, this man forced me to throw myself at his feet like a slave. He saw me detach from him, one by one the chains with which I had loaded him—and this man who knows our secrets, who has seen me thus, who can expose us, this man had the impudence to ask a rendezvous with me—a rendezvous at the Tower of Nesle! I still hesitated, but it was very impudent, right? It was tempting God! At least he invited himself—it's one less thing to be remorseful about.

ORSINI

Well, still one more. All I ask from you is some rest. I am the first to say "it must be done."

MARGUERITE

Ah—it has to be done, doesn't it, Orsini? You see, indeed, you also want him to die even if I didn't order you; for your own security, you would strike him?

ORSINI

Yes, yes, but a truce later; if your heart isn't yet satiated. Our iron will deaden and this will be enough, it will be too much for our eternal repose.

MARGUERITE

Yes, but our tranquility in this world demands it. So long as that man lives, I will not be Queen; I will not be mistress, neither of my power, nor my treasure, nor my life, but with him dead—Oh, I swear it to you, no more nights spent outside the Louvre, no more orgies in the Tower, no more bodies in the Seine. There I will give you enough gold to buy a province, and you will be free to return to your beautiful Italy or to remain in France. Listen, I will raze the tower; I will build a convent on its place; I will endow a community of monks and they will pass their lives praying on naked feet on naked stone; a prayer for me and a prayer for you for I tell you, Orsini, I am as weary as you of all these orgies and massacres—and it seems to me that God will pardon me for them if I weren't adding the last murder.

ORSINI

He knows our secrets, he can expose us. Which way is he going to come?

MARGUERITE

By this stairway.

ORSINI

After him, no others?

MARGUERITE

By the Blood of Christ! I swear it to you.

ORSINI

I am going to place my men.

MARGUERITE

Listen! Don't you see anything?

ORSINI

A bark containing two men.

MARGUERITE

One of these men—it's him. There is no time to lose—go, go—but shut this door—so that he cannot come to me. I can't, I don't wish to see him. Perhaps, he still has some secret which would save his life. Go, go—and shut me in.

(Orsini leaves.)

MARGUERITE

Ah! Gaultier, my beloved gentleman! He tried to separate us, this man. To separate us after what we were to each other. If he had only wanted gold, I would have given it to him; if honors, he should have had them—but he wanted to separate us, and he dies. Oh, if you knew that he wished to separate us, Gaultier, you yourself would pardon me his death. Oh! This Lyonnet, this Buridan, this demon, let him go back to Hell, where he came from. It's to you that I owe all my crimes. It's he who made me spill all this blood. Oh—if God is just, everything will fall back on him. And I, oh! I, I, if I was my own judge. I don't know if I would dare to absolve myself.

(she listens at the door)

I don't hear anything yet—nothing.

LANDRY

(at the foot of the tower)

Are you there?

BURIDAN

(from the balcony)

Yes.

MARGUERITE

Someone at the window—! Ah.

(Buridan breaks the window pane and comes in.)

MARGUERITE

(recoiling)

Help! Help!

BURIDAN

Don't be afraid.

MARGUERITE

You! You! Coming through this window, it's an apparition, a phantom.

BURIDAN

Don't fear, I tell you.

MARGUERITE

But why by this window and not by the door?

BURIDAN

I will tell you soon, but above all, I must speak to you; each moment lost is a treasure thrown in a gulf. Hear me.

MARGUERITE

Have you come again to threaten me, to impose some new condition?

BURIDAN

No, no, you have nothing to fear. Here, look—my sword and dagger are far from me—this box which contains our secrets as well. Now, you can kill me, I have no arms, or armor—kill me and take this box, burn it—and sleep tranquilly on my fall—oh, if you knew what I have to tell you! What days of happiness remain to us, to us who are so cruelly cursed.

MARGUERITE

Speak, I don't understand you.

BURIDAN

Marguerite, does nothing remain in your heart, nothing of a woman, nothing of a mother?

MARGUERITE

What are you getting at?

BURIDAN

Is the woman I once knew when she was so pure no longer accessible to what is sacred to God and men?

MARGUERITE

Is it you who wish to speak to me of virtues and purity! Satan, who makes conversions. It's strange, you must agree.

BURIDAN

Little matter what name, you give me, since my words don't

touch you. Marguerite have you never had an instance of repentance? Oh! Answer me as you would answer to God—I can do anything now for your joy or your despair—! I can damn you or absolve you. I can, at your choice, open heaven or hell to you. Suppose nothing had happened between us these last three days—forget everything except your old confidence towards me. Don't you need to tell someone all you have suffered?

MARGUERITE

Oh! Yes, yes, for there is no priest to whom one would dare confide such secrets! It is only an accomplice—and you are mine; of all my crimes! Yes, Buridan—or rather Lyonnet, yes, all my crimes stem from my first fault. If the young girl had not failed you, disastrously, in her duties, her first crime, the most horrible, would not have been committed. For no one suspected me of the death of my father, I lost my children. Pursued by remorse, I sought refuge in crime. I wanted to strangle the voice of my conscience in blood and pleasures for it cried to me incessantly "misfortune." Around me, not a word to recall me to virtue, the mouths of courtiers smiled at me, told me I was beautiful, that the world was mine, so that I could throw it over for a moment of pleasure. No strength to struggle. Some passions, some remorse; some nights full of ghosts, if they were not voluptuous. Oh—yes, yes—it is only to an accomplice that one can say such things.

BURIDAN

But tell me, so nearby you, you had your sons.

MARGUERITE

Oh! Then, had I dared, under their eyes, when the voice of my children had reminded me of my mother! Oh, had my children escaped me, they had returned me to virtue. But I could not keep my sons! My sons! But I could not keep my sons! My sons! Oh, I dared not pronounce these words—! For among the ghosts I had seen, I had not seen my sons—and I in calling them, to evoke their shades.

BURIDAN

Unfortunate mother! They were near you—and nothing told you, "Marguerite here are your sons."

MARGUERITE

Nearby me?

BURIDAN

One of the two, unfortunate mother, one of the two, you saw at your knees, begging mercy against the dagger of assassins. You were there, you heard his prayers—and you didn't recognize your child, and you said, "Strike!"

MARGUERITE

Me! Me! Where was that?

BURIDAN

Here—at this very place where we are.

MARGUERITE

Ah! When?

BURIDAN

Day before yesterday.

MARGUERITE

Philippe D'Aulnay? The vengeance of God!

BURIDAN

That's what has become of one, Marguerite, think who is the other?

MARGUERITE

Gaultier?

BURIDAN

The lover of his mother!

MARGUERITE

Oh, no, no—grace of heaven, this isn't it, and I thank God, I thank him on my knees. No, no, I can yet call Gaultier my son, and Gaultier can call me his mother.

BURIDAN

Do you speak the truth?

MARGUERITE

By the blood of the martyr which spilled here, I swear it to you. Oh, yes, yes, it's the hand of God that directs all this—who put in my heart this bizarre love, of a mother and not of a lover—! It's God! God, the Good God, the Savior who wills that with repentance joy will return to my life! Oh my God, thanks! Thanks!

(She prays.)

BURIDAN

Well, Marguerite, do you pardon me? Do you still see me as an enemy?

MARGUERITE

Oh! No, no, the father of Gaultier!

BURIDAN

Thus, you see it, we can still be happy—! Our ambitious are fulfilled, no more struggle between us. Our son is the chain that attaches us to each other. Our secret will be kept between us three!

MARGUERITE

Yes. Yes.

BURIDAN

Do you believe we can still be happy?

MARGUERITE

Oh! Yes, I believe it, and for ten minutes now I've hoped for nothing more.

BURIDAN

A single thing is lacking to our happiness, right?

MARGUERITE

Our son, our son there, between the two of us—our Gaultier.

BURIDAN

He's coming.

MARGUERITE

What?

BURIDAN

I gave him the key you gave to me. He's coming by this stairway, by which I should have come.

MARGUERITE

Curses! Because I was waiting for you—I placed—damnation—I placed some assassins in your passage.

BURIDAN

I recognize your well there, Marguerite.

(They hear a scream on the stairway.)

MARGUERITE

It's him they are strangling.

BURIDAN

Let's run—!

(They go to the door and struggle to open it.)

MARGUERITE

Who has barred this door? Oh! I did it. I did it! Orsini! Orsini! Don't strike! Misfortune!

BURIDAN

Door of hell! My son! my son!

MARGUERITE

Gaultier!

BURIDAN

Orsini! Demon! Hell! Orsini!

MARGUERITE

Pity! Pity!

GAULTIER

(outside)

Help! Help! To me!

MARGUERITE

The door is opening!

(She recoils.)

GAULTIER

(entering, covered with blood)

Marguerite! Marguerite! I bring you back the key to the Tower.

MARGUERITE

Misfortune, misfortune! I am your mother!

GAULTIER

My mother? Well—Mother—be cursed!

(He falls and dies.)

BURIDAN

(bending over his son and falling on his knees)

Marguerite—Landry made on each of them a mark on the left arm.

(he tears Gaultier's sleeve and looks at his arm)

You see it, it is indeed them—children damned at the breast of their mother. A murderer presided over their birth, a murderer has abridged their lives.

MARGUERITE

Mercy! Mercy!

(Orsini with Savoisy and the guards enter.)

ORSINI

(between two guards who hold him)

Milord, these are the true assassins—it's them and not me.

SAVOISY

You are my prisoners.

MARGUERITE and BURIDAN

Us—prisoners?

MARGUERITE

Me, the Queen?

BURIDAN

Me, the Prime Minister?

SAVOISY

Here there is neither Queen or Prime Minister; there is a body, two assassins, and an order signed by the King to arrest whoever they may be that I find here tonight in the Tower of Nesle.

CURTAIN

ABOUT THE AUTHOR

Frank J. Morlock has written and translated many plays since retiring from the legal profession in 1992. His translations have also appeared on Project Gutenberg, the Alexandre Dumas Père web page, Literature in the Age of Napoléon, Infinite Artistries.com, and Munsey's (formerly Blackmask). In 2006 he received an award from the North American Jules Verne Society for his translations of Verne's plays. He lives and works in México.

www.ingramcontent.com/pod-product-compliance
Lightning Source LLC
LaVergne TN
LVHW041620070426
835507LV00008B/351